All About Tower of London: A Kid's Guide to England's Historic Fortress

Educational Books For Kids, Volume 24

Shah Rukh

Published by Shah Rukh, 2024.

While every precaution has been taken in the preparation of this book, the publisher assumes no responsibility for errors or omissions, or for damages resulting from the use of the information contained herein.

ALL ABOUT TOWER OF LONDON: A KID'S GUIDE TO ENGLAND'S HISTORIC FORTRESS

First edition. September 29, 2024.

Copyright © 2024 Shah Rukh.

ISBN: 979-8227142856

Written by Shah Rukh.

Table of Contents

Prologue

Welcome to the fascinating world of the Tower of London, one of the most iconic landmarks in England! Imagine a place that has been standing for almost a thousand years, filled with stories of kings, queens, prisoners, and even ghosts. The Tower of London isn't just an old building—it's a fortress, a royal palace, a prison, and even a zoo! It has witnessed moments of great celebration, tales of betrayal, and more than a few mysteries that still puzzle us today.

In this book, you'll journey back in time to discover the secrets hidden within the Tower's mighty stone walls. From the legendary ravens that protect the fortress to the glittering Crown Jewels, each chapter will take you on an adventure through history. You'll meet some of the most famous (and infamous) characters who called the Tower home, learn about daring escapes, and hear about some spooky ghost stories that will give you chills.

The Tower of London is more than just a building—it's a place where history comes alive! So, get ready to explore the wonders of this historic fortress and uncover the many treasures, secrets, and legends that make it so special. Let's dive into a world of kings and queens, knights and soldiers, all waiting for you behind the Tower's thick walls. Adventure awaits!

Chapter 1: The Building of the Tower of London

The building of the Tower of London is one of the most fascinating chapters in the history of England. The Tower has stood for nearly a thousand years, a massive stone fortress that has been central to the story of kings and queens, invasions, battles, imprisonments, and the protection of treasures. It was initially built as a symbol of power and authority, serving as a stronghold for the ruling monarch and a clear warning to potential invaders or rebels.

The origins of the Tower of London date back to the time of William the Conqueror. After his victory at the Battle of Hastings in 1066, William I became the first Norman king of England. One of his main concerns was securing his new kingdom. He understood that in order to maintain control over the land and its people, he needed to build a strong, intimidating fortress that would help establish his dominance and ward off threats from both foreign invaders and internal uprisings. In 1078, William commissioned the construction of what would later become the White Tower, the most iconic part of the Tower of London complex.

The White Tower was the first part of the Tower of London to be constructed, and it still stands at the heart of the fortress today. Built on the north bank of the River Thames, the location was carefully chosen for both its defensive capabilities and its proximity to the city of London, which was the economic and political center of the country. The structure was intended to be both a royal palace and a defensive stronghold, and its thick stone walls, high towers, and narrow windows made it an almost impregnable fortress. The White Tower was constructed of Caen stone, which was imported from Normandy, as well as local Kentish stone, and its design followed the typical Norman style of fortifications, known for their square keeps. It was four stories tall, with walls up to 15 feet thick at the base, providing formidable protection against any attackers.

Inside the White Tower, the layout included a chapel, living quarters, and storage rooms. The design was intended to be both functional and impressive, reflecting the power and wealth of the king. The chapel, known as St. John's Chapel, is one of the finest examples of Norman architecture in England, with its rounded arches and simple, elegant design. This chapel was where kings and other important figures could worship, and it further emphasized the Tower's role as both a residence and a symbol of royal authority.

As time passed, the Tower of London expanded. Successive kings added to the original White Tower, building new walls, towers, and buildings to enhance its defenses and accommodate the changing needs of the monarchy. By the reign of King Richard the Lionheart in the late 12th century, the Tower had grown significantly. Richard added a moat to improve the fortress's defenses and further isolate it from potential attackers. The moat was fed by the River Thames, making it a watery barrier that added an additional layer of protection to the already heavily fortified walls. In the 13th century, King Henry III undertook significant construction projects to transform the Tower into a royal residence, while still maintaining its defensive function. Henry added luxurious apartments, gardens, and even a zoo, which housed exotic animals such as lions and elephants, gifts from foreign rulers. The Tower was becoming more than just a fortress; it was also a royal palace and a symbol of England's growing importance on the world stage.

However, it was under the reign of King Edward I, Henry's son, that the Tower of London reached its most formidable state as a fortress. Edward was a military-minded king who recognized the need to fortify the Tower even further. He built additional walls, creating a concentric design that enclosed the original White Tower and earlier structures within a series of defensive walls. This made the Tower almost impossible to breach, as attackers would have to penetrate multiple layers of fortifications to reach the heart of the fortress. Edward also improved the moat, reinforcing it with a system of water gates and defensive towers that could be manned by archers. Under Edward's reign, the Tower of London became the most secure fortress in all of England, a place where the king could retreat in times of danger and a visible reminder of his power over the kingdom.

The Tower of London continued to be modified and expanded in the centuries that followed, although its role evolved over time. By the 16th century, it was no longer used as a royal residence but had taken on new functions, such as serving as a prison, a treasury, and a storehouse for weapons and military supplies. The infamous Bloody Tower was where prisoners were held, including important figures such as Anne Boleyn, one of Henry VIII's wives, who was executed within the Tower's walls. Despite these changes in function, the Tower retained its symbolic importance as a fortress and a place of power.

The Tower also played a significant role in the defense of London during the medieval period. Its strategic location near the River Thames allowed it to control access to the city by water, and its massive walls and imposing towers made it a key point of defense in times of war or rebellion. The Tower has been involved in many important events in English history, including the Peasants' Revolt in 1381, when a group of rebels stormed the Tower and killed several officials, and the Wars of the Roses in the 15th century, when it was used as a refuge by both sides of the conflict.

In addition to its military and political importance, the Tower of London has also been a place of significant cultural and social influence. As a royal residence, it hosted important state ceremonies and events, and its architecture and design reflected the changing tastes and styles of different periods in English history. The Tower was also home to the Crown Jewels, which were kept there for safekeeping. The Crown Jewels remain in the Tower to this day, attracting millions of visitors from around the world who come to see the dazzling symbols of British monarchy.

Today, the Tower of London stands as a testament to nearly a millennium of English history. It has witnessed the rise and fall of kings and queens, the triumphs and tragedies of the nation, and the changing roles of monarchy and government. Its massive stone walls and towers tell the story of a time when castles and fortresses were central to the survival of kingdoms, and its continued preservation allows future generations to experience the grandeur and history of this remarkable fortress. From its beginnings as a Norman stronghold to its current status as a UNESCO World Heritage Site, the Tower of London remains one of the most iconic and enduring symbols of England's history.

Chapter 2: The Crown Jewels of the Tower

The Crown Jewels of the Tower of London are among the most iconic and precious treasures in the world, representing centuries of British history, monarchy, and tradition. These magnificent pieces are not just symbols of royal power and wealth but also hold significant cultural, ceremonial, and religious importance. The collection, stored securely within the Jewel House at the Tower of London, contains some of the most famous and valuable regalia used in the coronation of monarchs, as well as other ceremonial occasions, and has been central to the British monarchy for hundreds of years.

The history of the Crown Jewels is deeply intertwined with the history of the British monarchy. While some elements of the collection date back to ancient times, the current Crown Jewels mostly reflect the monarchy's history from the late medieval period onward. Many of the original medieval treasures were destroyed in the mid-17th century, during the English Civil War, when the monarchy was temporarily overthrown, and England became a republic under Oliver Cromwell. The monarchy was restored in 1660 with the coronation of King Charles II, and a new set of Crown Jewels was created for the occasion. Much of what we see today was made following this restoration, though some pieces were retained or replicated from earlier times.

The most famous and recognizable items in the collection are the crowns themselves, each of which plays a specific role in the coronation ceremony or other royal events. Perhaps the most famous crown is St. Edward's Crown, which has been used in the coronation of British monarchs for centuries. St. Edward's Crown is a large, gold crown that is adorned with jewels and has a distinctive cross design at the top. It weighs about 2.23 kilograms (nearly five pounds), making it quite heavy for the monarch to wear during the ceremony. This crown was originally made for the coronation of Charles II in 1661, replacing the original medieval crown that had been destroyed after the English Civil War. It is traditionally only worn at the moment of crowning, during the coronation itself, as it is considered a sacred and highly symbolic item. The crown takes its name from Edward the Confessor, the Anglo-Saxon king who was canonized as a saint, and it has become one of the most important symbols of the British monarchy.

Another significant crown in the collection is the Imperial State Crown, which is worn by the monarch during the State Opening of Parliament and other important occasions. The Imperial State Crown is slightly lighter than St. Edward's Crown, but it is no less spectacular. It is set with over 3,000 precious stones, including some of the most famous jewels in the world. Among these is the Cullinan II diamond, also known as the Second Star of Africa, which is one of the largest diamonds ever discovered. The crown also features the Black Prince's Ruby, an enormous red spinel that has been part of the Crown Jewels since the 14th century, as well as the Stuart Sapphire and the St. Edward's Sapphire, both of which have historic and symbolic connections to the British royal family. The crown's design, with its arches, cross, and fleur-de-lis, symbolizes the monarch's role as both the head of state and the defender of the faith.

In addition to the crowns, the Crown Jewels collection includes other important items of regalia that are used during coronation ceremonies and other royal events. One of the most significant of these is the Sovereign's Sceptre with Cross, a golden rod that represents the monarch's temporal power and authority. The sceptre is adorned with the Cullinan I diamond, also known as the Great Star of Africa, which is the largest clear-cut diamond in the world, weighing an astounding 530 carats. This diamond alone makes the sceptre one of the most valuable and recognizable pieces in the Crown Jewels. The sceptre is held by the monarch during the coronation ceremony, symbolizing their rule over the land and their responsibilities as sovereign. The sceptre's design includes intricate goldwork and jewels, making it one of the most visually striking items in the collection.

Another important piece is the Sovereign's Orb, a golden globe surmounted by a cross, which represents the monarch's religious authority and the Christian world. The orb is set with hundreds of precious stones and is a key part of the coronation ceremony, symbolizing the divine right of kings and queens to rule. The monarch holds the orb during the coronation as a reminder of their sacred duty to govern according to the will of God and the laws of the land. The orb, like the sceptre, is a powerful symbol of the monarch's dual role as both a political leader and a spiritual figurehead.

The collection also includes several swords, each of which plays a specific role in the coronation ceremony. The Sword of State, for example, represents the monarch's duty to protect the realm and uphold justice. It is carried before the monarch during the coronation procession and is a reminder of the king or queen's role as the leader of the nation's armed forces. Another important sword is the Sword of Offering, which is presented to the monarch during the ceremony as a symbol of their willingness to defend the faith and the people of their kingdom. These swords, like the crowns and sceptres, are richly decorated with gold, jewels, and intricate designs, reflecting their importance in the ceremony and the symbolism they carry.

In addition to the crowns, sceptres, orbs, and swords, the Crown Jewels collection also includes a number of other important items used in royal ceremonies. These include the Coronation Spoon, which dates back to the 12th century and is used during the anointing of the monarch with holy oil, a sacred part of the coronation ceremony. The spoon is one of the oldest items in the collection, having survived the destruction of the original Crown Jewels during the English Civil War. Its continued use in coronation ceremonies today highlights the deep historical connections between the monarchy and the Christian faith.

The Crown Jewels also contain numerous other ceremonial items, such as trumpets, maces, and rings, each of which plays a specific role in royal ceremonies. For example, the coronation ring, also known as the "Wedding Ring of England," is placed on the monarch's hand during the coronation as a symbol of their union with the nation. The regalia also includes various chalices, plates, and other items used in religious services and state banquets.

One of the most fascinating aspects of the Crown Jewels is their role in British history. The collection has witnessed some of the most significant events in the monarchy's history, from coronations and state openings of Parliament to times of crisis and celebration. The Crown Jewels were famously under threat during World War II, when they were secretly hidden in the Tower of London to protect them from potential bombing raids. Today, they are displayed in the Jewel House at the Tower of London, where millions of visitors from around the world come to marvel at their beauty and learn about the rich history they represent.

The Crown Jewels are not only valuable because of their historical and ceremonial significance but also due to the sheer value of the materials they are made from. The diamonds, sapphires, rubies, and other precious stones that adorn the regalia are some of the most famous and valuable in the world. The Cullinan diamonds, in particular, are among the largest and most extraordinary gems ever discovered, and their presence in the Crown Jewels adds to the collection's allure and mystique. These jewels are more than just objects of beauty; they are symbols of the power, continuity, and legacy of the British monarchy.

In conclusion, the Crown Jewels of the Tower of London are a stunning collection of regalia that have been used for centuries in the coronation of British monarchs and other important state ceremonies. They are a testament to the grandeur and tradition of the British monarchy, representing the authority, wealth, and responsibility of the sovereign. From the glittering crowns set with priceless gems to the golden sceptres and orbs that symbolize the monarch's power and faith, the Crown Jewels are a remarkable legacy of the nation's royal heritage. Today, they continue to captivate and inspire, standing as one of the most iconic and enduring symbols of British royalty.

Chapter 3: Famous Prisoners Held in the Tower

The Tower of London has long been infamous for its role as one of the most feared prisons in British history. While the Tower today is a popular tourist destination, its past is steeped in tales of imprisonment, intrigue, and death. Over the centuries, many high-profile figures, including monarchs, nobles, religious leaders, and political dissidents, were imprisoned within its imposing walls. Some of these prisoners were subjected to torture, some were executed, and others lived under strict confinement, knowing their freedom and lives were in jeopardy. The stories of these famous prisoners offer a glimpse into the turbulent history of the English monarchy and the political struggles that shaped the nation.

One of the most famous early prisoners of the Tower of London was Ranulf Flambard, who became the first recorded prisoner held in the Tower in 1100. Flambard, the Bishop of Durham, had been a key advisor to William II (Rufus) but fell out of favor after the king's death. Imprisoned on charges of extortion, Flambard made a daring escape from the Tower by using a rope smuggled into his cell inside a wine cask. His successful flight from the Tower set the tone for future stories of intrigue and adventure, though many prisoners were not so lucky.

Perhaps the most infamous royal prisoners held in the Tower were the two young sons of King Edward IV, known as the Princes in the Tower. Edward V and his younger brother, Richard of Shrewsbury, Duke of York, were sent to the Tower in 1483 by their uncle, Richard, Duke of Gloucester, who claimed responsibility for their safety. The boys, aged 12 and 9, were never seen again. Their mysterious disappearance has been the subject of intense speculation and debate for centuries, with many historians believing that Richard, who became King Richard III, was responsible for their deaths in order to secure his own claim to the throne. The exact fate of the princes remains one of the greatest unsolved mysteries of English history. The princes' story has inspired countless books, plays, and films, making them two of the most famous prisoners ever held in the Tower.

One of the most tragic stories associated with the Tower is that of Anne Boleyn, the second wife of King Henry VIII. Anne's marriage to Henry had changed the course of English history, as Henry broke from the Catholic Church and established the Church of England in order to divorce his first wife, Catherine of Aragon, and marry Anne. However, the once-passionate relationship between Henry and Anne quickly soured when Anne failed to produce a male heir. In 1536, Anne was arrested and imprisoned in the Tower on charges of adultery, treason, and incest. After a swift and controversial trial, she was found guilty and sentenced to death. On May 19, 1536, Anne Boleyn was executed by beheading at the Tower's scaffold, becoming one of the most famous prisoners to meet her end within its walls. Anne's tragic fall from grace has captivated historians and the public alike for centuries, and her ghost is said to haunt the Tower to this day, particularly near the Chapel of St. Peter ad Vincula, where she is buried.

Another one of Henry VIII's wives, Catherine Howard, also met her fate in the Tower. Catherine, the king's fifth wife, was arrested in 1541, accused of committing adultery with Thomas Culpeper, a courtier, and of engaging in a premarital relationship with Francis Dereham. Like Anne Boleyn, Catherine was taken to the Tower of London, where she awaited her execution. On February 13, 1542, Catherine was beheaded on the same spot where Anne had been executed. She was buried in an unmarked grave in the Chapel of St. Peter ad Vincula. The tragic fates of Henry VIII's queens highlight the perilous position of women at the Tudor court, where political intrigue and personal ambitions often led to deadly consequences.

The Tower of London was also the site of imprisonment and execution during the turbulent reign of Mary I, Henry VIII's daughter by his first wife, Catherine of Aragon. Known as "Bloody Mary" due to her persecution of Protestants, Mary imprisoned her half-sister, Elizabeth, in the Tower in 1554. Mary, a devout Catholic, feared that Elizabeth, who had Protestant sympathies, was involved in a plot to overthrow her and take the throne. For two months, Elizabeth was held in the Tower under suspicion of treason. Though she was eventually released, her time in the Tower was a constant reminder of the political danger she faced. When Mary died in 1558, Elizabeth succeeded her to the throne and became one of England's greatest monarchs, ruling for 45 years as Queen Elizabeth I. The story of Elizabeth's imprisonment is often seen as one of survival, resilience, and the shifting fortunes of royalty in a time of religious and political conflict.

Perhaps one of the most famous military leaders to be imprisoned in the Tower was Sir Thomas More, a close advisor to Henry VIII who later became one of the king's most prominent critics. More, a devout Catholic, refused to acknowledge Henry as the Supreme Head of the Church of England, leading to his arrest and imprisonment in 1534. Despite his long-standing loyalty to the king, More was accused of treason for refusing to take the Oath of Supremacy, which recognized Henry's authority over the church. More's trial was highly publicized, and his steadfast refusal to abandon his principles ultimately led to his execution. He was beheaded at the Tower in 1535, and his death is remembered as a martyrdom in both Catholic and Protestant histories. More's story continues to be celebrated for its defense of individual conscience in the face of absolute power, and his legacy as a writer and philosopher endures to this day.

The Tower of London's role as a prison extended beyond the Tudor period, playing a significant part in later political upheavals, such as the English Civil War. One of the key figures imprisoned in the Tower during this time was William Laud, the Archbishop of Canterbury, who was a staunch supporter of King Charles I. Laud's attempts to enforce Anglican religious practices were deeply unpopular with many, particularly among the Puritans, who saw him as a symbol of royal overreach. He was arrested in 1640 and imprisoned in the Tower for several years before being executed in 1645. His imprisonment and death were part of the larger conflict between the monarchy and Parliament, which eventually led to the execution of Charles I and the temporary abolition of the monarchy.

During the 17th century, the Tower of London also held many political prisoners, especially in the aftermath of failed rebellions and uprisings. One of the most notable was Guy Fawkes, the conspirator behind the Gunpowder Plot of 1605. Fawkes and a group of Catholic extremists plotted to blow up the Houses of Parliament in an attempt to assassinate King James I and restore Catholic rule in England. However, their plan was foiled, and Fawkes was captured. He was imprisoned in the Tower, where he was tortured to reveal the names of his fellow conspirators. Fawkes and his co-conspirators were executed for treason, but his legacy lives on in British culture. Every year on November 5th, "Guy Fawkes Night" is celebrated with fireworks and bonfires to commemorate the failure of the Gunpowder Plot.

In more modern times, the Tower of London was used as a prison during World War I and World War II. Notably, during World War I, several spies for Germany were held at the Tower before being executed by firing squad. Perhaps the most famous of these was Carl Hans Lody, a German naval officer who was arrested for espionage in 1914. He became the first person to be executed at the Tower in over 150 years, highlighting the Tower's enduring role as a place of punishment for those who threatened the security of the nation. Similarly, during World War II, Rudolf Hess, a high-ranking Nazi official, was imprisoned in the Tower after his mysterious flight to Scotland in 1941. Although Hess was not executed, his imprisonment in the Tower marked one of the last times the fortress was used to house high-profile prisoners.

The stories of the Tower of London's prisoners reflect the complex and often brutal history of England, where political power struggles, religious conflicts, and dynastic rivalries frequently resulted in imprisonment, torture, and execution. The Tower's reputation as a place of fear and foreboding is well-earned, with its dark history echoing through the centuries. From monarchs and queens to military leaders, religious martyrs, and political rebels, the Tower has held some of the most famous and influential figures in English history within its walls. Today, the Tower stands as a symbol of the resilience and endurance of the monarchy and the nation, its legacy enriched by the stories of those who once called it their prison.

Chapter 4: The Legend of the Ravens

The Legend of the Ravens at the Tower of London is one of the most fascinating and enduring tales associated with this ancient fortress. These black-feathered birds have become an integral part of the Tower's identity, steeped in history, superstition, and mystery. According to the legend, the presence of ravens at the Tower is not just a charming tradition but a vital safeguard for the British monarchy and the nation itself. The belief is that as long as the ravens remain at the Tower, the kingdom will stand; if they ever leave, the Tower will crumble and a great disaster will befall England.

The origins of the legend are unclear, but the association of ravens with the Tower can be traced back several centuries. Ravens have long been seen as mysterious and supernatural creatures in folklore across many cultures. In Norse mythology, for example, Odin, the god of wisdom, war, and death, had two ravens, Huginn and Muninn, who flew around the world and brought him information. In Celtic lore, ravens were often linked to death, warfare, and prophecy, and were seen as omens of both good and bad fortune. In the Tower of London, these dark birds took on a unique significance, blending ancient myth with the historical role of the Tower as a royal fortress, prison, and symbol of power.

The story of the Tower ravens became widely known in the 19th century, although it may have older roots. One of the most popular versions of the legend suggests that it was King Charles II in the 17th century who decreed that the ravens must always remain at the Tower. The tale goes that astronomer John Flamsteed, who had established an observatory in the Tower before Greenwich Observatory was built, complained to the king that the ravens were interfering with his astronomical observations. In response, Charles II ordered that the birds be removed. However, before this could be carried out, the king was warned by his advisors that if the ravens were ever to leave the

Tower, both the monarchy and the Tower would fall. Taking this warning seriously, Charles II is said to have decreed that at least six ravens must always be kept at the Tower, ensuring the protection of both the crown and the country.

Though this particular story is widely circulated, historical evidence for Charles II's involvement in the ravens' protection is scant, and it is more likely that the tradition evolved over time, combining elements of myth and royal superstition. What is clear, however, is that by the 19th century, the presence of ravens at the Tower had become an established tradition, and the legend of their vital role in preserving the monarchy had taken hold.

Today, the ravens are considered official residents of the Tower of London, and they are cared for by a special guardian known as the Ravenmaster, a position within the Yeoman Warders (commonly known as Beefeaters). The Ravenmaster's duties include feeding, monitoring, and looking after the wellbeing of the ravens, ensuring that they remain healthy and do not stray too far from the Tower. The role of Ravenmaster is a prestigious and unique responsibility, one that involves deep respect for the birds as living symbols of British heritage.

The Tower of London is home to at least six ravens at any given time, in accordance with the supposed decree of Charles II. In fact, to ensure the safety of the kingdom, there are usually seven or more ravens kept at the Tower, with one or two serving as spares in case any of the birds become ill or fly away. Each raven is carefully named and known to both the Ravenmaster and the public. Over the years, individual ravens have gained their own personalities and fan followings, with some becoming minor celebrities in their own right. They are allowed to roam freely around the Tower grounds, though one of their wings is lightly clipped to prevent them from flying too far away. Despite this, some ravens have been known to wander beyond the Tower's walls or even disappear altogether, leading to great concern among the Tower's staff and the British public.

The disappearance of a raven has, in fact, caused alarm on several occasions. In 2013, a raven named Munin went missing from the Tower, sparking fears that the legendary curse might come true. After days of searching, the Ravenmaster and the Tower staff concluded that Munin had flown away and was unlikely to return. Though Munin's fate remained a mystery, another raven was soon brought to the Tower to replace her, ensuring that the required number of ravens remained on duty. Incidents like this feed into the mystique surrounding the ravens and their perceived importance to the nation.

The care and training of the Tower's ravens are taken very seriously, and the birds enjoy a privileged lifestyle. They are fed a diet of fresh meat, biscuits soaked in blood, and even an occasional treat of raw eggs, all designed to keep them in optimal health. The ravens are also given plenty of attention and stimulation to keep them active and engaged. They are known to be highly intelligent birds, capable of solving problems and interacting with humans in playful and sometimes mischievous ways. Ravens are also social animals and can form strong bonds with the Ravenmaster and other Tower staff.

Despite their sometimes playful and curious nature, the ravens have a darker side that reflects their traditional association with death and mystery. Ravens are carrion birds, meaning they often feed on dead animals, which has historically linked them to death and the supernatural. Their black plumage, sharp beaks, and distinctive cawing calls add to their eerie reputation. In medieval times, ravens were often seen around battlefields and execution sites, feeding on the bodies of the fallen, further cementing their image as harbingers of doom and death. Given the Tower of London's own bloody history as a site of executions and imprisonments, it is fitting that ravens have become such an integral part of its folklore.

The Tower's ravens are also closely associated with British royal pageantry and tradition. They often feature in ceremonies, military parades, and royal events held at the Tower, further enhancing their symbolic status. In recent years, the ravens have become a major draw for tourists visiting the Tower, many of whom are eager to see these legendary birds and hear the stories about their role in safeguarding the monarchy. Visitors are often surprised by the size of the ravens, which are much larger than common crows, and they are fascinated by the birds' intelligence and curiosity.

Despite the legend's more ominous elements, the ravens are generally seen today as positive symbols of continuity and resilience. They have witnessed countless historical events at the Tower, from royal coronations and state banquets to imprisonments and executions. Their continued presence at the Tower is a reminder of England's deep historical roots and the endurance of its traditions. The ravens have become a living link between the ancient past and the modern era, embodying both the Tower's long history and its place in the national consciousness.

The ravens' role in British culture extends beyond the Tower itself. The birds have become symbols of London and the monarchy, appearing in literature, art, and popular culture. They are often referenced in poems, stories, and films that explore themes of power, mystery, and the supernatural. For example, Edgar Allan Poe's famous poem "The Raven" invokes the bird as a symbol of death and loss, though Poe's raven is a solitary and tragic figure, whereas the Tower's ravens represent resilience and survival. The ravens have also appeared in numerous films, TV shows, and novels that depict the Tower of London and its rich history, further cementing their place in popular imagination.

In conclusion, the Legend of the Ravens at the Tower of London is much more than just a quaint tradition or a tourist attraction. It is a powerful symbol that links the monarchy, the Tower, and the nation's history to a deeper cultural mythology of protection, continuity, and mystery. The ravens, with their ancient associations with death and prophecy, have taken on a unique role at the Tower, blending folklore with royal superstition. The presence of these birds at the Tower has become an enduring reminder of the Tower's long and often dark history, while also serving as a living connection to England's royal past. Today, the Tower ravens continue to fascinate and intrigue, drawing millions of visitors each year who are eager to see these legendary guardians of the realm and learn about the stories that surround them. Their presence ensures that, for now at least, the Tower stands strong, and the monarchy endures.

Chapter 5: The Tower's Role in the Middle Ages

The Tower of London played a crucial and multifaceted role during the Middle Ages, serving as a fortress, royal palace, prison, treasury, and symbol of power. Its imposing presence on the north bank of the River Thames became a focal point of political, military, and social life in medieval England. Constructed shortly after the Norman Conquest of 1066, the Tower's significance grew over the centuries as monarchs expanded and strengthened it to serve their needs. The Tower's central position in English history during the Middle Ages reflects the turbulent nature of the period, marked by invasions, rebellions, political intrigue, and the constant need to assert royal authority.

The origins of the Tower of London date back to the reign of William the Conqueror, who became the first Norman king of England after defeating the Anglo-Saxon king Harold II at the Battle of Hastings in 1066. William faced resistance from the Anglo-Saxon nobility, and to secure his hold on the newly conquered territory, he built a series of castles across England. One of the most important of these fortresses was the Tower of London, intended to assert Norman power over London, the country's largest and wealthiest city, and to protect against potential uprisings or invasions. The White Tower, the central keep of the Tower of London, was constructed between 1078 and 1100 and became the core of the entire complex.

During the early Middle Ages, the Tower served primarily as a military stronghold, ensuring that William and his successors could maintain control over London. Its strategic location near the river allowed for quick resupply and reinforcement in the event of an attack, and its formidable walls and towers made it difficult to breach. The Tower's defensive capabilities were tested during several conflicts, including during the reign of King Stephen in the 12th century when

England was embroiled in a civil war known as "The Anarchy." The Tower, held by supporters of Stephen's rival, Empress Matilda, became a key point of contention in the struggle for control of the English throne.

As England's political landscape evolved, so too did the Tower's role. It was not only a fortress but also a royal residence where monarchs and their families could retreat for safety in times of unrest. The Tower was outfitted with luxurious accommodations fit for royalty, including a great hall, private chambers, and a chapel. King Henry III, who reigned from 1216 to 1272, was particularly fond of the Tower and spent considerable time and money improving its defenses and adding to its aesthetic appeal. He commissioned the construction of a royal chapel, St. Peter ad Vincula, and added new buildings and walls to make the complex more imposing. Henry's son, Edward I, continued these efforts, transforming the Tower into an even more powerful fortress. He built a series of concentric walls around the original White Tower, creating a highly advanced defensive structure that could withstand prolonged sieges. The Tower's transformation under Henry III and Edward I reflected the growing need for monarchs to secure their hold on power during periods of political instability.

The Tower also functioned as a key administrative center for the monarchy during the Middle Ages. It housed the royal treasury, which was essential for funding the king's wars, building projects, and lavish lifestyle. The Crown Jewels were stored at the Tower, symbolizing the wealth and power of the English monarchy. The Tower's treasury was carefully guarded, and throughout the medieval period, its role as a financial hub made it vital to the functioning of the kingdom. The Tower's role as a repository for royal wealth extended to its use as a mint, where coins were produced under the strict control of the crown. The importance of maintaining the integrity of the currency during this period meant that the Tower's mint was a closely guarded operation.

Perhaps one of the most notorious roles the Tower of London played during the Middle Ages was that of a prison. The Tower became the site of imprisonment for high-profile captives, including members of the nobility, political enemies, and even royals. During times of political upheaval or rebellion, the Tower served as a place where the crown could incarcerate those who posed a threat to the monarchy. The medieval period was rife with political rivalries, and the Tower became a place where intrigue, betrayal, and power struggles played out behind its stone walls.

One of the most famous prisoners held in the Tower during the Middle Ages was Ranulf Flambard, the Bishop of Durham, who was imprisoned in 1100. His daring escape from the Tower, using a rope hidden in a wine cask, became the first recorded prison break from the Tower. Over time, the Tower gained a reputation for housing prisoners of immense political significance. During the reign of King John, who ruled from 1199 to 1216, political opponents and rebellious barons were often imprisoned there as the king sought to strengthen his power over the realm. These tensions came to a head with the signing of the Magna Carta in 1215, which limited the king's authority and granted more rights to his barons. The Tower of London was deeply involved in this period of conflict, standing as both a symbol of royal power and a tool for suppressing dissent.

In addition to political prisoners, the Tower also held religious prisoners during the Middle Ages. This was particularly evident during periods of religious turmoil, such as the reign of Henry III, when the tension between the monarchy and the Church was high. The Tower housed figures who had fallen afoul of the crown for religious reasons, and it played a significant role in the enforcement of royal authority over the church. The imprisonment of religious figures reflected the broader struggle between the monarchy and the church over matters of governance, land ownership, and influence.

The Tower of London's role as a prison reached its zenith during the Wars of the Roses, a series of dynastic conflicts that took place in the latter half of the 15th century. The wars were fought between the rival houses of Lancaster and York, both of which claimed the right to the English throne. The Tower played a critical role in this period of political instability, as it became the site of imprisonment and execution for many key figures in the conflict. Perhaps the most infamous episode during this time was the disappearance of the Princes in the Tower, Edward V and his younger brother Richard, Duke of York, who were sent to the Tower in 1483 by their uncle, Richard, Duke of Gloucester. The boys were never seen again, and their fate remains one of the greatest mysteries in English history. Many historians believe that they were murdered in the Tower to secure Richard's claim to the throne, though no definitive proof has ever been found. This dark chapter added to the Tower's reputation as a place of intrigue, treachery, and death.

Beyond its political and military functions, the Tower of London also served as a center of social life and spectacle during the Middle Ages. The Tower was a site of royal ceremonies, banquets, and tournaments, where the nobility gathered to celebrate and display their wealth and power. The Tower's role in hosting these grand events further underscored its importance as a symbol of royal authority. The Tower was not just a place of imprisonment and fortification but also a venue for demonstrating the grandeur of the monarchy. Royal coronations, weddings, and other significant events were often marked by processions that included the Tower, emphasizing its connection to the crown.

The Tower's role as a place of execution also became infamous during the medieval period. Although many executions took place at Tower Hill, just outside the fortress, some of the most high-profile executions were carried out within the Tower's walls, particularly those of members of the nobility or royals. Executions were public spectacles that drew large crowds and served as a grim reminder of the consequences of treason or rebellion against the crown. The Tower's proximity to the execution site reinforced its reputation as a place of death and punishment.

As the medieval period progressed, the Tower of London continued to expand and evolve, reflecting the changing needs of the monarchy and the kingdom. By the end of the Middle Ages, the Tower had grown into a massive complex of walls, towers, gates, and buildings that served multiple functions. It remained a military stronghold, royal palace, prison, and treasury, but it also became a symbol of the continuity of the monarchy. The Tower's endurance through centuries of conflict, rebellion, and political change made it a powerful emblem of the monarchy's resilience.

The Middle Ages were a time of great change in England, marked by shifting political alliances, religious conflict, and the constant threat of invasion or rebellion. Throughout these turbulent centuries, the Tower of London stood as a bastion of royal power and authority, its walls bearing witness to the rise and fall of kings, queens, and nobles. The Tower's role during this period was not static but dynamic, adapting to the needs of the monarchy and the challenges of the time. Whether as a fortress, a royal residence, a prison, or a place of spectacle, the Tower of London remained at the heart of England's medieval history. Its enduring presence in the political and social life of the kingdom made it one of the most important and iconic structures of the Middle Ages.

Chapter 6: The Execution of Anne Boleyn

The execution of Anne Boleyn is one of the most infamous and poignant events in English history. As the second wife of King Henry VIII and the mother of Queen Elizabeth I, Anne's life was intertwined with political intrigue, religious upheaval, and the personal ambitions of the Tudor monarchy. Her execution on May 19, 1536, at the Tower of London, marked the tragic end of a queen whose rise to power had been meteoric but whose downfall was equally swift and brutal. The story of her execution is not only a tale of personal tragedy but also a reflection of the broader dynamics of power, religion, and gender in the court of Henry VIII.

Anne Boleyn's rise to prominence began in the early 1520s when she returned to England from France, where she had served in the court of Queen Claude, the wife of Francis I. Her charm, wit, and sophistication quickly caught the eye of Henry VIII, who was already growing disillusioned with his first wife, Catherine of Aragon. Catherine had failed to produce a male heir, and Henry, desperate to secure the Tudor dynasty, became infatuated with Anne. Unlike many women at court, Anne refused to become the king's mistress, insisting that she would only accept marriage. This decision set in motion a series of events that would lead to the English Reformation and ultimately to Anne's tragic fate.

Henry's desire to marry Anne led him to seek an annulment of his marriage to Catherine, a request that was refused by the Pope. Frustrated by the Pope's refusal, Henry took matters into his own hands, leading to a dramatic break with the Roman Catholic Church. In 1533, he declared himself the Supreme Head of the Church of England, effectively creating a new religious order in England. This act, known as the English Reformation, allowed Henry to annul his marriage to Catherine and marry Anne Boleyn in a secret ceremony in January 1533. Anne was crowned queen in a lavish coronation ceremony in June of that same year.

At first, Anne's position seemed secure. She was pregnant with Henry's child, and the king was confident that she would give birth to the long-awaited male heir. However, in September 1533, Anne gave birth to a daughter, the future Queen Elizabeth I. Although Henry was disappointed, he continued to hope that Anne would provide him with a son. Over the next few years, Anne suffered several miscarriages, and her failure to produce a male heir began to undermine her position at court. Henry, whose affections were notoriously fickle, began to tire of Anne and turned his attention to one of her ladies-in-waiting, Jane Seymour.

As Anne's relationship with Henry deteriorated, her enemies at court, who had long resented her influence and her role in the break with Rome, began to plot her downfall. Chief among these enemies was Thomas Cromwell, Henry's chief minister, who had once been a supporter of Anne but had fallen out with her over matters of policy and power. Cromwell, sensing that Henry was losing interest in Anne, saw an opportunity to remove her from power and consolidate his own position.

In early 1536, a series of accusations were leveled against Anne, accusing her of treason, adultery, and even incest with her own brother, George Boleyn, Viscount Rochford. These charges were shocking, particularly the accusation of incest, which was considered one of the most heinous crimes in Tudor society. The charges also included allegations that Anne had engaged in adulterous relationships with multiple courtiers, including Henry Norris, a close friend of the king, and Mark Smeaton, a musician. These accusations, whether true or fabricated, were enough to convince Henry to proceed with her trial and execution.

Anne was arrested on May 2, 1536, and taken to the Tower of London, where she was imprisoned in the Queen's Lodgings, the same apartments she had stayed in before her coronation. Despite the gravity of the charges against her, Anne maintained her innocence throughout her imprisonment and trial. She was given a trial on May 15, 1536, before a jury of peers, including her uncle, the Duke of Norfolk, and other prominent noblemen. The outcome of the trial was a foregone conclusion, as Henry had already decided that Anne must be removed from power to make way for Jane Seymour.

The trial was a highly charged and dramatic affair, with Anne defending herself with remarkable eloquence and dignity. However, the evidence against her, much of which was likely fabricated or exaggerated, was damning. The most sensational charge was the accusation of incest with her brother George, a claim that shocked and appalled the court. Despite her eloquent defense, Anne was found guilty of all charges, including treason, adultery, and incest. The sentence was death, to be carried out either by burning at the stake or by beheading, depending on the king's mercy.

On May 17, 1536, two days before her execution, Anne watched as her brother George Boleyn and several other men accused of adultery with her were executed on Tower Hill. This was a particularly cruel blow, as Anne was deeply close to her brother, and his death added to the emotional torment of her final days. Anne herself was scheduled to be executed on May 18, but her execution was postponed by one day. Some historians speculate that this delay was intended to give Anne time to reflect on her fate or perhaps to allow Henry to finalize his plans for her successor, Jane Seymour.

On the morning of May 19, 1536, Anne Boleyn was led to the scaffold erected on Tower Green, within the Tower of London. Her execution was to be a private affair, witnessed by a small group of courtiers and officials, rather than a public spectacle on Tower Hill. The decision to conduct the execution within the Tower walls was likely made to minimize the potential for unrest or scandal, as Anne had been a queen and her fall from grace was still fresh in the minds of the public.

Anne's execution was carried out by an expert French swordsman, a rare act of mercy granted by Henry. In England, beheadings were typically done with an axe, which could result in a brutal and botched execution if the executioner was not skilled. By contrast, the use of a sword was considered a quicker and more humane method of execution, and it was usually reserved for nobility or royalty. The swordsman had been specially brought from France for the occasion, and his presence ensured that Anne's final moments would be as swift and dignified as possible.

Before her execution, Anne delivered a final speech that has been remembered for its composure and grace. She did not openly protest her innocence, likely recognizing that such a statement would do little to change her fate. Instead, she acknowledged her position as a queen and expressed loyalty to the king, asking God to have mercy on her soul. Her speech, though brief, reflected the complex emotions of a woman who had risen to the highest ranks of power only to be brought down in a matter of weeks. It also demonstrated her awareness of the political reality she faced — that challenging the king or the court at this moment would have no effect on the outcome.

Anne knelt on the scaffold, and in a swift and precise movement, the swordsman beheaded her. Her body and head were placed in an arrow chest and buried in an unmarked grave in the Chapel of St. Peter ad Vincula within the Tower of London, where many other executed prisoners were laid to rest. Anne's death marked the end of one of the most dramatic and controversial chapters in the reign of Henry VIII. Within days, Henry was betrothed to Jane Seymour, and the court moved on quickly from Anne's downfall. The speed with which Henry remarried suggests that Anne's execution had been carefully planned to facilitate the king's new marriage and his ongoing quest for a male heir.

The execution of Anne Boleyn had profound implications for England and for Henry VIII's reign. It marked a turning point in the king's personal and political life, as he continued to reshape the religious and political landscape of the country to suit his needs. Anne's fall from grace also served as a warning to others at court, particularly women, about the dangers of crossing the king or failing to meet his expectations. Her death demonstrated the precarious nature of power in Tudor England, where even a queen could be brought down by the whims of a volatile monarch.

In the centuries that followed, Anne Boleyn's life and death became the subject of intense debate and speculation. Many historians have questioned the validity of the charges against her, with some suggesting that the accusations were part of a carefully orchestrated plot by Cromwell and other political enemies to remove her from power. Others have pointed to the possibility that Henry himself believed the charges, as he sought to rid himself of a wife who had failed to produce a male heir. Whatever the truth, Anne's execution remains one of the most controversial events in English history.

In popular culture, Anne Boleyn has been portrayed in various ways, from a tragic victim of Henry's ambition to a manipulative and ambitious woman who brought about her own downfall. Her legacy is inextricably linked to that of her daughter, Queen Elizabeth I, who would go on to become one of England's greatest monarchs. In this sense, Anne's greatest legacy was not her short and tumultuous reign as queen but her role as the mother of a future queen who would define an era.

The execution of Anne Boleyn remains a powerful symbol of the dangers of absolute power, the complexities of royal politics, and the personal tragedies that often unfolded behind the grandeur of the Tudor court. It serves as a reminder of the harsh realities of life at the court of Henry VIII, where loyalty and favor could shift in an instant, and where even the most powerful figures could find themselves facing the executioner's blade. Today, Anne Boleyn's story continues to captivate and intrigue, offering a window into the fascinating and often brutal world of Tudor England.

31

Chapter 7: Ghost Stories from the Tower

The Tower of London, with its nearly thousand-year history, has been the setting for countless tragic, violent, and mysterious events, making it a prime location for ghost stories. The eerie atmosphere of this ancient fortress, where some of England's most notorious prisoners were held, tortured, and executed, provides a fitting backdrop for tales of hauntings and spectral apparitions. Throughout the centuries, numerous visitors, guards, and residents of the Tower have reported encountering strange phenomena, claiming to have seen the restless spirits of historical figures who met tragic ends within its walls. These ghost stories are an inseparable part of the Tower's lore, offering a glimpse into the darker, more supernatural side of its long and storied past.

One of the most famous and enduring ghost stories associated with the Tower of London involves Anne Boleyn, the ill-fated second wife of King Henry VIII. Anne's execution in 1536 is one of the Tower's most infamous events, and her ghost is said to haunt several parts of the fortress. According to legend, Anne Boleyn's headless spirit has been seen wandering the Tower Green, the site of her execution, and the Chapel of St. Peter ad Vincula, where she is buried. Witnesses have claimed to see her ghostly figure, sometimes holding her severed head, walking through the corridors or standing by the altar in the chapel. Her restless spirit is said to be trapped within the Tower, a reflection of the tragic and unjust nature of her death. Some stories even suggest that Anne's ghost has been spotted in the White Tower, the oldest part of the complex, as if she is forever bound to the place where her life ended so dramatically.

The ghost of Anne Boleyn is not the only royal specter said to haunt the Tower. The two young princes, Edward V and his brother Richard, Duke of York, are also believed to roam the fortress where they disappeared under mysterious circumstances. In 1483, the two boys were sent to the Tower by their uncle, Richard, Duke of Gloucester, who would later become Richard III. They were never seen again, and many historians believe that they were murdered, likely on Richard's orders, to secure his claim to the throne. In the centuries since their disappearance, numerous people have reported seeing the ghostly figures of two small boys dressed in nightclothes, wandering the grounds of the Tower or standing hand-in-hand near the Bloody Tower, where they were believed to have been killed. The spectral presence of the Princes in the Tower is often described as melancholic and tragic, with the boys seemingly unaware of their fate, forever lost within the walls of the fortress where their young lives were cut short.

Another famous ghost story from the Tower of London centers around Lady Jane Grey, the "Nine Days' Queen." Lady Jane was an unfortunate pawn in a political struggle for the English throne, crowned queen in 1553 after the death of Edward VI. Her reign lasted only nine days before she was overthrown by Mary I, also known as "Bloody Mary." Jane was imprisoned in the Tower and, after being convicted of treason, was executed on February 12, 1554, at the age of just 16. The young and tragic figure of Lady Jane has long been associated with the Tower, and her ghost is said to appear in the area near the Queen's House, where she was held before her execution. Some witnesses have described seeing a pale, sorrowful figure dressed in Tudor-style clothing, standing near the site of her death or gazing out of the windows of the Tower. Her ghost is often regarded as a symbol of innocence betrayed, and the poignancy of her story has ensured that her spirit remains one of the most famous and enduring presences within the Tower's walls.

The White Tower, the central and oldest building of the Tower of London, has its own share of ghost stories. Built by William the Conqueror in the 11th century, the White Tower has stood for nearly a millennium, its stone walls bearing witness to countless events in England's history. One of the most chilling ghost stories associated with the White Tower involves the spirit of a huge bear. In the 19th century, a sentry on duty at the Tower claimed to have seen the apparition of a massive bear charging towards him. The soldier was so terrified by the encounter that he reportedly died of shock soon afterward. This strange sighting has been linked to the Tower's history as a menagerie, where exotic animals, including bears, lions, and elephants, were kept as part of the royal collection. While the menagerie was long gone by the time the ghost bear was reportedly seen, the lingering presence of such a creature has added to the Tower's reputation as a place where the past, both human and animal, refuses to rest.

Another spectral figure said to haunt the Tower is the ghost of Sir Walter Raleigh. A famous courtier, writer, and explorer during the reign of Elizabeth I, Raleigh was imprisoned in the Tower several times over the course of his life, the last time for treason against King James I. After years of imprisonment, Raleigh was executed in 1618. However, his ghost is said to have remained behind in the Tower, particularly in the area known as the Bloody Tower, where he was held for many years. Raleigh's ghost is often described as dignified and contemplative, appearing as if he is deep in thought, perhaps reflecting on his long and troubled career or his ultimate betrayal. Some reports suggest that his spirit is seen walking along the battlements of the Tower, gazing out over the River Thames, as though still dreaming of the adventures he would never again undertake.

The Tower's long association with imprisonment, torture, and execution has also given rise to stories of disembodied cries and the sounds of footsteps echoing through the darkened corridors. The Torture Chamber, located within the Tower, is said to be a particularly haunted area, with many visitors reporting feelings of intense unease or hearing strange noises, such as the rattling of chains or the groaning of prisoners in agony. The shadowy figure of a gaunt man, possibly one of the many unfortunate souls tortured here, is occasionally glimpsed moving through the gloom. The dark and oppressive atmosphere of the Torture Chamber serves as a chilling reminder of the brutal methods used to extract confessions or punish prisoners during the Tower's long history as a prison.

One of the lesser-known but equally eerie ghost stories involves the ghost of Margaret Pole, Countess of Salisbury. Margaret was a member of the Plantagenet family and a relative of the Tudors, but her loyalty to the Catholic Church and her opposition to Henry VIII's religious reforms led to her arrest and eventual execution in 1541. Her death, however, was particularly brutal and chaotic. Margaret, who was in her late sixties, was not beheaded cleanly; the inexperienced executioner botched the job, and she was hacked to death in a gruesome spectacle. Her ghost is said to haunt the Tower Green, where she was executed, and many claim to have seen her running frantically, as if trying to escape her grim fate. The sight of her restless spirit re-enacting her final moments has contributed to the Tower's reputation as a place where the past comes to life in the most terrifying ways.

The ghost stories of the Tower of London are not limited to famous historical figures; many of the fortress's more anonymous prisoners are also said to haunt its ancient halls. For centuries, the Tower was used as a prison for commoners and nobility alike, and it was the site of numerous executions, both public and private. Visitors to the Tower have reported hearing ghostly voices, footsteps, and even the sounds of weeping coming from the cells and dungeons where prisoners were once held. Some have claimed to feel unseen hands brush against them, or to sense an inexplicable chill in the air, particularly in areas like the Salt Tower, where prisoners were often kept in isolation for years at a time. These anonymous spirits, though less well-known than the likes of Anne Boleyn or Lady Jane Grey, are a testament to the Tower's long and often brutal history as a place of imprisonment and punishment.

Beyond the Tower's walls, even the nearby Tower Hill, the site of many public executions, is said to be haunted. The ghost of Thomas

More, the famous scholar and statesman who was executed in 1535 for refusing to acknowledge Henry VIII as the Supreme Head of the Church of England, is said to appear on the hill, still dressed in his execution clothes. More's ghost is often seen standing solemnly, as if awaiting his final judgment. His stoic and dignified presence contrasts with the more tragic and violent hauntings associated with the Tower, but his spirit, like those of so many others, is said to be forever tied to the place where his life came to a sudden and unjust end.

The Tower of London's ghost stories have been passed down through generations, and they continue to captivate and terrify those who visit this historic fortress. Whether rooted in historical fact, embellished by centuries of legend, or simply the product of overactive imaginations, these tales of restless spirits and unexplained phenomena add to the Tower's mystique. The sheer volume of ghost stories associated with the Tower reflects its deep connection to England's turbulent past, where power struggles, betrayal, and execution were part of everyday life. The ghosts of the Tower are more than just figures of folklore; they represent the human cost of ambition, betrayal, and the relentless pursuit of power that defined so much of England's history. As long as the Tower of London stands, it seems likely that stories of its ghostly inhabitants will continue to capture the imagination of those who visit its ancient halls.

Chapter 8: The Tower's Moat and Defenses

The Tower of London, one of the most iconic and formidable fortresses in England, has stood for nearly a thousand years, safeguarding the heart of the nation. A key aspect of its defense system was its moat, a wide, watery barrier that encircled the Tower and helped protect it from attack. The moat, along with the fortress's imposing walls, bastions, and towers, formed a formidable defensive system that deterred enemies and secured the Tower as a symbol of royal power and authority. The history of the Tower's moat and defenses is a fascinating tale of architectural ingenuity, military strategy, and adaptation to the changing technologies of warfare over the centuries.

When William the Conqueror began building the Tower of London in the late 11th century, his primary goal was to establish a stronghold that would not only protect the city of London but also assert Norman dominance over England. The original structure, the White Tower, was a massive stone keep, designed to be both a royal residence and a military stronghold. However, as the Tower grew in size and importance, so did the need for more extensive defenses. By the 13th century, under the reign of King Henry III and his son, King Edward I, the Tower of London had been expanded to include multiple layers of fortifications, including the iconic moat that became a crucial part of its defensive system.

The Tower's moat, often referred to as a ditch in medieval records, was initially a dry ditch when it was first constructed. However, during the reign of King Edward I in the late 13th century, the moat was transformed into a wet moat. Edward was a master of castle building, having fortified many castles across Wales and England, and he understood the importance of a water-filled moat in providing an additional layer of defense. A wet moat would make it much more difficult for attackers to approach the walls, as they would need to cross a wide and deep body of water, often under fire from archers stationed on the walls above.

Edward ordered the construction of a moat around the Tower that would be filled with water from the nearby River Thames. This work was part of a broader project to enhance the Tower's defenses, including the construction of new walls, towers, and gates. The new wet moat was a significant engineering achievement. It was designed to be around 50 meters wide in places and over 10 feet deep, encircling the entire complex. The moat would have made it extremely difficult for enemy soldiers to get close to the Tower's outer walls, as they would have had to deal not only with the water but also with the danger of drowning, as well as attacks from defenders on the battlements above.

The moat's defensive capabilities were further enhanced by the use of drawbridges and fortified gates. The Tower had several gates, including the Byward Gate and the Bloody Tower Gate, both of which were heavily fortified and protected by portcullises, iron gates that could be lowered to block entry. The drawbridges could be raised to prevent access across the moat, effectively sealing off the Tower from potential invaders. The most famous gate of the Tower, the Traitors' Gate, was also connected to the moat and the River Thames. This gate was used to bring prisoners into the Tower by boat, and its name became infamous because so many high-profile prisoners, including Anne Boleyn and Sir Thomas More, passed through it on their way to imprisonment or execution.

In addition to the moat and the gates, the Tower's walls were an essential part of its defense system. The outer curtain wall, which encircled the entire complex, was built to withstand attacks from both siege engines and artillery. The wall was strengthened with several towers, including the Bell Tower, the Wakefield Tower, and the Salt Tower, which provided lookout points and places for archers and soldiers to defend the fortress. These towers also served as places of imprisonment for high-ranking captives, further emphasizing the Tower's dual role as both a royal palace and a prison.

The moat itself, however, was not without its challenges. Over time, the water quality in the moat deteriorated, and it became more of a stagnant cesspool than a clean, flowing waterway. The moat was fed by the River Thames, but the tidal nature of the river meant that water could flow in and out of the moat at different times, bringing with it silt and debris. By the 16th century, the moat had become a breeding ground for disease, and its defensive value was diminished. During the reign of Queen Elizabeth I, efforts were made to clean the moat, but the problem persisted.

As warfare evolved during the late medieval and early modern periods, the Tower's defenses had to adapt. The development of gunpowder and artillery in the 14th and 15th centuries brought about significant changes in military strategy and castle design. The high stone walls that had once been effective against attackers with swords and arrows were now vulnerable to cannon fire. To counter this, additional bastions and gun platforms were added to the Tower's defenses, allowing for the placement of cannons and other artillery. These platforms, such as the Brass Mount and the Legge's Mount, were designed to provide overlapping fields of fire, creating a more effective defensive perimeter.

Despite these upgrades, the Tower of London never faced a full-scale siege during the Tudor or Stuart periods. However, its reputation as an impregnable fortress and the symbolic power it held as the seat of royal authority helped deter any serious attempts to capture it. The moat and defenses served as both a practical and psychological barrier, reminding would-be attackers of the consequences of challenging the monarchy.

The Tower's defenses, including the moat, also played a role in more ceremonial and symbolic functions. During times of royal processions, such as coronations or other state events, the Tower would often be a focal point, with its moat and walls decorated to reflect the grandeur of the monarchy. The moat, once a place of grim defense, also became a backdrop for royal pageantry, reinforcing the Tower's role as both a fortress and a symbol of the crown.

By the 18th century, the Tower of London's role as a military fortress was beginning to wane, and its defensive features, including the moat, were no longer considered essential in the face of modern warfare. However, the moat remained an iconic feature of the Tower's landscape. In the 19th century, as part of a broader effort to modernize and clean up the Tower, the moat was finally drained. This decision was made in part because of the poor condition of the water and the health risks it posed to those living and working in the Tower. Once the moat was drained, it was transformed into open space, and parts of it were later used for gardens and ceremonial purposes.

The drained moat, though no longer filled with water, still served as a reminder of the Tower's long and defensive history. During World War II, the Tower of London was once again called into service as a military stronghold, though its role was largely symbolic. The moat, having been drained for centuries, was used for air-raid shelters and other practical purposes during the war, further highlighting the Tower's enduring importance to London's history.

In the 21st century, the Tower of London's moat has become a central part of the visitor experience. Though it no longer serves as a defensive barrier, it continues to play a role in shaping the Tower's identity as one of the most important historic sites in the United Kingdom. In recent years, the moat has been used for special exhibitions and events, including the famous "Ceremony of the Poppies" in 2014, which commemorated the centenary of World War I. The installation, titled "Blood Swept Lands and Seas of Red," filled the moat with hundreds of thousands of ceramic poppies, each representing a British or colonial soldier who died during the war. This poignant display transformed the moat into a sea of red, a powerful reminder of the sacrifices made during the war and the Tower's continuing role as a symbol of national memory.

In summary, the Tower of London's moat and defenses played a crucial role in the history of the fortress. From its origins as a dry ditch to its transformation into a water-filled moat under Edward I, the moat served as a powerful deterrent against attackers and a key part of the Tower's defensive system. Alongside its walls, towers, gates, and artillery, the moat helped protect the Tower and the city of London from potential invaders for centuries. While the Tower's military significance declined in later centuries, the moat remained a potent symbol of the fortress's strength and endurance. Today, though it no longer serves a defensive purpose, the moat continues to be an important part of the Tower's landscape, a reminder of its long and storied past.

Chapter 9: The Life of a Beefeater

The life of a Beefeater, officially known as a Yeoman Warder, is one steeped in history, tradition, and an unmistakable sense of duty. These iconic figures, clad in their distinctive uniforms of red and gold or dark blue and red, have been guarding the Tower of London for centuries. Their presence at this historic fortress is more than just ceremonial; Beefeaters are custodians of the Tower's stories, traditions, and, most famously, the Crown Jewels. To become a Beefeater is to step into a world of rigid protocols, fascinating history, and an extraordinary role that blends the past and present. A Beefeater's life is rich with responsibilities that range from guiding visitors through the Tower's ancient halls to performing ceremonial duties that go back hundreds of years. Each day as a Beefeater is unique, but every action is shaped by a deep respect for the history they protect and the legendary institution they represent.

To understand the life of a Beefeater, one must first appreciate the centuries-old tradition from which the role originates. The Yeoman Warders were established by King Henry VII in 1485, making them one of the oldest continuous military corps in the world. The origins of the term "Beefeater" are less clear. Some believe it refers to their position as royal bodyguards, who had the privilege of eating as much beef as they wished from the king's table. Others suggest it might come from the French word "buffetier," which referred to guards of the king's food. Whatever the origin, the name Beefeater has stuck, and today it is synonymous with the warders who guard the Tower of London. Over the centuries, the role of the Beefeaters has evolved, but their central purpose remains the same: to protect the Tower, its treasures, and the people who live within its walls.

To become a Beefeater is not an easy task. In fact, the criteria for joining the ranks are quite strict. All Beefeaters must be former senior non-commissioned officers in the British Armed Forces, having served a minimum of 22 years. In addition, they must have been awarded the Long Service and Good Conduct Medal. This means that every Beefeater has an extensive military background, often having served in challenging roles or even in combat zones. Their military experience equips them with the discipline, knowledge, and commitment required to fulfill their duties at the Tower. Once accepted, new Beefeaters must undergo a rigorous training process to prepare them for their unique responsibilities. They need to learn the Tower's history, master the various ceremonies they will take part in, and familiarize themselves with the expectations of their role.

One of the primary roles of a Beefeater is to serve as a guide for the millions of tourists who visit the Tower of London each year. Beefeaters are the storytellers of the Tower, sharing its dramatic and often grim history with visitors from around the world. Their tours are a highlight for many visitors, and Beefeaters are known for their engaging storytelling, dry humor, and deep knowledge of the Tower's history. They recount tales of famous prisoners held in the Tower, including Anne Boleyn and Lady Jane Grey, and they guide visitors through the various towers, gates, and chambers that make up this ancient fortress. But more than just providing historical information, Beefeaters bring the Tower's past to life, blending facts with legends to create a rich, immersive experience for those who visit.

Yet, the life of a Beefeater is not just about guiding tourists. There is a serious ceremonial aspect to their duties as well. One of the most important and iconic responsibilities of the Beefeaters is guarding the Crown Jewels, which are housed in the Jewel House within the Tower. These priceless symbols of the British monarchy include crowns, scepters, orbs, and other regalia used in coronations and state events. The Beefeaters work alongside the Royal Household Guards to ensure that these treasures are protected at all times. This duty requires constant vigilance, as the Crown Jewels are among the most valuable and historically significant items in the world. Beefeaters must be on high alert, as the security of the Tower and its precious contents depends on them.

In addition to guarding the Crown Jewels, Beefeaters also play a key role in one of the oldest and most important nightly ceremonies in the Tower's history: the Ceremony of the Keys. This ancient ritual, which has been performed every night for over 700 years, marks the formal locking of the Tower's gates. The ceremony takes place precisely at 9:53 p.m., and it is carried out with a precise, time-honored protocol. During the ceremony, the Chief Yeoman Warder, accompanied by the Tower's military escort, locks the heavy gates of the Tower with a ceremonial key. As the gates are locked, a challenge is issued: "Who comes there?" The response is always the same: "The Keys." The ceremony ends with the call of "God preserve the King!" or "God preserve the Queen!" depending on the reigning monarch. This ritual, though short, is a powerful reminder of the Tower's role as a royal fortress, and it underscores the Beefeaters' duty to protect the Tower and its inhabitants.

Living in the Tower of London is another unique aspect of a Beefeater's life. Unlike most historic landmarks, the Tower is not just a museum; it is a working community. Beefeaters, along with their families, live within the walls of the Tower itself. The Yeoman Warders' living quarters are located in the Tower's inner precincts, providing them with a rare and privileged lifestyle. They live in a place steeped in history, surrounded by ancient stone walls, and they share this space with a small but vibrant community of people who work at the Tower, including the Tower's Governor and some of the military personnel. Living at the Tower means that Beefeaters are constantly immersed in the history and traditions they protect. It also allows them to form a close-knit community with their fellow Beefeaters and their families.

Despite the many privileges of living and working at such a historic site, being a Beefeater is not without its challenges. The role is highly demanding, both physically and mentally. Beefeaters spend much of their day on their feet, walking around the Tower's vast grounds, giving tours, and performing their ceremonial duties. They must be constantly aware of their surroundings, as they are responsible for the security of one of the most important sites in the United Kingdom. In addition, Beefeaters are often called upon to participate in high-profile events and state occasions, which require them to maintain a high level of professionalism and decorum at all times. The ceremonial aspects of their role, including the wearing of their elaborate uniforms, can also be physically demanding, especially during the summer months when the Tower is at its busiest.

The Beefeater uniform itself is an iconic part of their identity. There are two types of uniforms that Beefeaters wear, depending on the occasion. The everyday uniform is a dark blue and red outfit, which is worn during regular duties such as guiding tours or standing guard. This uniform is relatively simple, but it still carries the weight of history, with the royal monogram (currently "E II R" for Queen Elizabeth II, though this will eventually change for King Charles III) prominently displayed. The more elaborate ceremonial uniform is worn on state occasions and special events. This uniform is a striking red and gold outfit, complete with a ruff collar and a large, flat hat. The ceremonial uniform is a throwback to the Tudor period and is instantly recognizable to anyone familiar with the Tower of London. Wearing these uniforms is a point of pride for Beefeaters, as they symbolize their role as protectors of the Tower and its traditions.

One of the most cherished traditions associated with the Beefeaters is their connection to the Tower's famous ravens. Legend has it that if the ravens ever leave the Tower of London, the kingdom will fall. As a result, the ravens are considered an essential part of the Tower's history and mystique. Beefeaters are responsible for caring for the ravens, feeding them and ensuring their well-being. This responsibility is taken very seriously, and there is even an official Yeoman Warder Ravenmaster, whose sole duty is to look after the Tower's resident ravens. The ravens have become as much a symbol of the Tower as the Beefeaters themselves, and they are a constant presence, both for the Yeoman Warders and the visitors who come to the Tower.

The life of a Beefeater is not just about guarding the Tower and its treasures; it is also about embodying the living history of the Tower of London. Each Beefeater is a walking connection to the past, representing centuries of royal service, military tradition, and national pride. Their role is both symbolic and practical, blending the ceremonial with the everyday. Beefeaters are not only guardians of the Tower but also ambassadors for British history, sharing the stories of the Tower's famous prisoners, its dramatic sieges, and its royal ceremonies with visitors from around the world. The unique combination of history, tradition, and duty makes the life of a Beefeater one of the most fascinating and respected roles in the British military and royal household.

In conclusion, the life of a Beefeater is a blend of military discipline, historical responsibility, and public service. These men and women are more than just ceremonial figures; they are the living embodiment of the Tower of London's rich and complex history. From guarding the Crown Jewels to performing the ancient Ceremony of the Keys, from guiding thousands of visitors through the Tower's storied past to caring for the Tower's ravens, the life of a Beefeater is one of dedication, tradition, and pride. Living within the walls of one of the most famous fortresses in the world, Beefeaters are not only protectors of the Tower but also its keepers, ensuring that its legacy endures for future generations.

Chapter 10: The Tower's Secret Tunnels

The Tower of London, one of the most iconic and historic landmarks in Britain, is renowned for its towering walls, its imposing structure, and its storied history that spans nearly a thousand years. While much of the Tower's rich history is well-documented, filled with tales of kings, queens, political intrigue, and even ghostly legends, there are some aspects of the fortress that remain shrouded in mystery. Among these are the Tower's secret tunnels, hidden passageways, and underground chambers, which have long been the subject of fascination, speculation, and legend. These tunnels, some real and some the product of centuries of myth, add another layer to the already complex and intriguing history of the Tower of London. The secretive and mysterious nature of these tunnels fuels imaginations, as they represent the unseen, the hidden, and the unknown aspects of the Tower's storied past.

The Tower of London, built initially by William the Conqueror in 1066, was designed to serve multiple purposes: a royal residence, a fortress to protect the city, and a prison for some of England's most infamous figures. The need for secrecy and security was paramount, and over time, the fortress was expanded and fortified with additional structures. As the Tower's role evolved, so too did the construction beneath it. Hidden tunnels and passageways were often constructed to ensure the safety of royals, provide escape routes in times of siege, or secretly move prisoners or treasure in and out of the Tower without detection. These tunnels, along with their rumored purposes, have captivated historians, researchers, and visitors alike, offering a glimpse into a part of the Tower's history that remains largely unexplored.

One of the most famous and historically verified tunnels beneath the Tower of London is the one leading from the White Tower, the central keep, to the nearby River Thames. This tunnel is believed to have been used by royalty and nobility for discreet and secure passage into and out of the Tower, especially during times of conflict or political unrest. It would have allowed kings, queens, and high-ranking officials to leave the Tower by boat, escaping the notice of enemies or prying eyes. During medieval times, when the Tower was often the seat of power in London, controlling this tunnel was vital for ensuring the safety of the monarch and the continuity of governance. This tunnel is said to have been used by monarchs such as Henry VIII and his daughter, Elizabeth I, during moments of political tension. The idea that a monarch could escape or enter the Tower undetected adds to the romanticized notion of the Tower as a place of secrets and intrigue.

In addition to the verified tunnels, there are also numerous legends and rumors surrounding the existence of other secret passageways and chambers beneath the Tower. Some of these stories have been passed down through generations, becoming part of the Tower's folklore, while others are based on historical events and plausible scenarios. One persistent legend involves the idea of an underground tunnel leading from the Tower to Westminster, which was the seat of royal power for much of England's history. This tunnel, according to legend, would have allowed monarchs or high-ranking officials to move between the Tower and Westminster without being seen. While no archaeological evidence has definitively confirmed the existence of such a tunnel, the idea remains popular, and it speaks to the Tower's role as both a fortress and a political prison, where secrecy and control were paramount.

Another significant feature associated with the Tower's secret tunnels is the network of underground dungeons and holding cells that existed beneath various parts of the fortress. While these spaces were primarily used for holding prisoners, some historians believe that there may have been hidden passageways connected to these dungeons, which allowed for the movement of prisoners in and out of the Tower without public knowledge. These tunnels would have been especially useful during politically sensitive times, such as when high-profile prisoners, including members of the aristocracy or foreign dignitaries, were held within the Tower. The existence of such tunnels would have ensured that these prisoners could be transported to and from the Tower without causing public outcry or attracting attention from enemies. In this context, the tunnels would have served both as a means of controlling the flow of information and as a way to safeguard the Tower's high-profile detainees.

The Tower of London's history as a prison is well-documented, and its role in imprisoning some of the most famous figures in British history adds to the intrigue surrounding its secret tunnels. Notable prisoners, such as Anne Boleyn, Sir Thomas More, and Guy Fawkes, were held within the Tower's walls. Their fates were sealed within its dungeons and chambers, and it is easy to imagine how secret tunnels might have been used to transport these prisoners or smuggle them to their eventual executions or trials. The infamous Traitors' Gate, which opens onto the River Thames, is itself connected to the idea of secret and hidden passages. While Traitors' Gate is above ground and highly visible, it is believed that some prisoners may have been moved through concealed tunnels that led from the river to various parts of the Tower, avoiding public view and adding a layer of mystery to the already dark and foreboding atmosphere of the Tower's prison system.

One of the most tantalizing aspects of the Tower's secret tunnels is the possibility that some of these passageways have yet to be discovered or fully explored. The Tower of London is an incredibly complex structure, with layers of history built upon each other over the centuries. Archaeological investigations have uncovered portions of tunnels and underground chambers, but much of the Tower's underground network remains uncharted. The potential for undiscovered passageways adds an air of mystery to the Tower's already fascinating history. Some believe that there are hidden tunnels that were intentionally sealed off or forgotten, possibly containing artifacts, treasure, or even the remains of prisoners long since forgotten by history. The idea that beneath the Tower's stone walls lies a hidden labyrinth of tunnels and chambers waiting to be discovered fuels the imagination and continues to draw visitors and researchers to the site.

In addition to their practical uses, the Tower's secret tunnels have also played a role in the mythology and ghost stories associated with the fortress. The Tower of London is famously haunted, with numerous sightings of ghostly figures reported over the centuries. Some of these apparitions, such as the ghost of Anne Boleyn, are said to have been seen near or within the tunnels. The underground nature of the tunnels, combined with their dark history as potential routes for moving prisoners or conducting secretive activities, makes them a perfect setting for ghostly tales. The idea that spirits may linger in the tunnels, trapped by the secrecy and violence that once occurred there, adds to the eerie atmosphere that permeates the Tower of London. Whether or not one believes in ghosts, the connection between the tunnels and the Tower's haunted reputation is undeniable.

Throughout history, secret tunnels have often been used as a means of escape, and the Tower of London is no exception. One of the most famous escape attempts from the Tower involved a secret passageway, though in this case, it was above ground. In 1483, the young Edward V and his brother Richard, known as the Princes in the Tower, were imprisoned by their uncle, Richard, Duke of Gloucester (later Richard III). According to legend, the princes were secretly moved through a hidden passage and either smuggled out of the Tower or murdered. Their disappearance remains one of the great mysteries of English history, and while no definitive evidence of a tunnel connected to their escape or demise has been found, the legend persists. This story, like many others associated with the Tower's tunnels, blurs the line between historical fact and myth, creating a rich tapestry of intrigue that continues to captivate audiences.

In modern times, interest in the Tower's secret tunnels has led to various explorations and investigations, both historical and archaeological. Advances in technology, such as ground-penetrating radar and other non-invasive techniques, have allowed researchers to study the underground areas of the Tower in greater detail. Some discoveries have been made, including sections of tunnels that were previously unknown or forgotten, but much of the underground network remains a mystery. These ongoing investigations keep the legend of the Tower's tunnels alive, and each new discovery adds another layer to the Tower's already complex history.

The fascination with secret tunnels is not unique to the Tower of London, but the Tower's place in British history makes its tunnels particularly compelling. For centuries, the Tower was a symbol of royal power, political intrigue, and, at times, terror. The existence of hidden tunnels beneath such a storied fortress adds to the sense of mystery and reinforces the Tower's reputation as a place where secrets are kept, and dark deeds are done. The tunnels, whether real or imagined, represent the hidden side of history—the parts of the story that were never meant to be seen or known. As long as the Tower of London stands, the legend of its secret tunnels will continue to capture the imagination of those who visit, offering a tantalizing glimpse into the unknown.

In conclusion, the secret tunnels of the Tower of London are an integral part of its mystique and allure. While some tunnels are historically verified and others remain the stuff of legend, the idea of hidden passageways beneath the Tower speaks to our fascination with the unseen, the unknown, and the hidden aspects of history. These tunnels, whether used for escape, transport, or concealment, add another layer to the already rich and complex history of the Tower. They are a reminder that beneath the surface of history lies a world of secrets, waiting to be uncovered. Whether explored through historical research or simply imagined through stories and legends, the secret tunnels of the Tower of London remain one of its most enduring and intriguing mysteries.

Chapter 11: The Tower During the Tudor Era

The Tower of London during the Tudor era was one of the most significant and dramatic periods in the fortress's long history. Spanning the reigns of five monarchs—Henry VII, Henry VIII, Edward VI, Mary I, and Elizabeth I—the Tudor period was marked by intense political upheaval, religious reform, dynastic intrigue, and a series of high-profile imprisonments and executions. The Tower, as both a royal palace and a prison, played a central role in many of the most important events of the time. Its use as a symbol of power, a place of punishment, and a fortress of political control meant that the Tower was intricately connected to the changing fortunes of the Tudor monarchs, their courtiers, and those who found themselves on the wrong side of the monarchy.

At the beginning of the Tudor era, the Tower of London had already been a significant royal fortress for several centuries, but it was during the reign of Henry VII, the first Tudor king, that it took on new importance. Henry VII ascended to the throne after defeating Richard III at the Battle of Bosworth in 1485, ending the Wars of the Roses, a prolonged civil war between the houses of Lancaster and York. Henry's claim to the throne was somewhat tenuous, and he faced opposition from various Yorkist factions who continued to pose a threat to his rule. The Tower became a crucial tool in Henry's strategy to consolidate power. He used the Tower both as a residence and as a symbol of his authority, imprisoning key rivals and those suspected of disloyalty within its walls. One of the most notable events during Henry VII's reign was the imprisonment and eventual execution of Edward Plantagenet, the Earl of Warwick, who was seen as a legitimate Yorkist claimant to the throne. Warwick spent most of his life imprisoned in the Tower and was ultimately executed in 1499 to eliminate any threat to the Tudor dynasty.

The reign of Henry VII's son, Henry VIII, is perhaps the most well-known and transformative period in the Tower's history. Henry VIII is famous for his six marriages, his break with the Catholic Church, and his role in the English Reformation, all of which had direct consequences for the Tower of London. Henry's need for a male heir and his desire to assert absolute control over both the monarchy and the church led to a series of imprisonments, trials, and executions that shaped the Tower's legacy. The most infamous of these events was the execution of Anne Boleyn, Henry's second wife, in 1536. Anne, once a beloved queen, fell out of favor when she failed to produce a male heir and was accused of adultery, treason, and incest. After a swift trial, she was condemned to death and executed by beheading on Tower Green, a moment that has become one of the most iconic and tragic episodes in English history. Anne's fall from grace was a stark reminder of the Tower's role as a place where power could be lost in an instant, and where the monarch's word was absolute law.

Henry VIII's use of the Tower as a place of imprisonment for those who opposed his religious policies was also a defining aspect of his reign. Following his break from the Catholic Church and the establishment of the Church of England, Henry sought to eliminate any dissenters who remained loyal to the Pope. The Tower became a prison for many of these individuals, including high-ranking church officials, scholars, and members of the nobility who refused to recognize Henry's religious supremacy. One of the most notable prisoners during this period was Sir Thomas More, a former close advisor to Henry and a devout Catholic. More's refusal to accept Henry's authority as the head of the Church led to his imprisonment in the Tower in 1534. After spending more than a year in the Tower, More was tried for treason, found guilty, and executed in 1535. His martyrdom for his faith made him a symbol of resistance to the Tudor monarchy's religious policies, and his time in the Tower highlighted the fortress's role as a site of religious persecution during the Reformation.

In addition to its use as a prison, the Tower also continued to serve as a royal residence during Henry VIII's reign. Although Henry preferred other palaces, such as Hampton Court and Whitehall, the Tower remained an important ceremonial site. Henry VIII used the Tower for state occasions, including the coronations of his queens. Both Anne Boleyn and her successor, Jane Seymour, were crowned in ceremonies that involved spending the night before their coronation in the royal apartments of the Tower. These lavish coronation ceremonies underscored the Tower's enduring importance as a symbol of royal power and its connection to the monarchy. However, the grandeur of these ceremonies stood in stark contrast to the grim fate that awaited many of Henry's queens and courtiers who later found themselves imprisoned within the Tower's walls.

Following Henry VIII's death in 1547, the Tower continued to play a crucial role during the reigns of his three children: Edward VI, Mary I, and Elizabeth I. Each of these monarchs faced significant challenges during their reigns, and the Tower was often at the center of political and religious conflicts. Edward VI, Henry's only son, inherited the throne as a young boy, and his short reign was dominated by the regency of powerful nobles, many of whom sought to advance their own agendas. During this time, the Tower was used to imprison rivals and potential threats to Edward's authority. One of the most famous prisoners during Edward's reign was his own uncle, Thomas Seymour, who was accused of plotting to marry Edward's sister Elizabeth and take control of the government. Seymour was arrested, imprisoned in the Tower, and executed in 1549.

The Tower's role as a political prison continued during the reign of Mary I, Henry VIII's eldest daughter. Mary, a staunch Catholic, sought to reverse the Protestant reforms of her father and brother, leading to a period of intense religious conflict. The Tower became a prison for many Protestant leaders who opposed Mary's efforts to restore Catholicism in England. One of the most significant events during Mary's reign was the imprisonment of her younger sister, Elizabeth, who would later become Elizabeth I. Elizabeth was suspected of being involved in a Protestant rebellion against Mary's rule, and in 1554, she was imprisoned in the Tower. Elizabeth's imprisonment was a tense and dangerous time for the future queen, as she faced the very real possibility of execution. However, Elizabeth's political savvy and the lack of concrete evidence against her allowed her to survive her time in the Tower, and she was eventually released. Her experiences in the Tower would later shape her reign as queen, during which she would use the Tower to imprison her own political enemies.

When Elizabeth I ascended to the throne in 1558, the Tower of London remained a key instrument of power during her reign. Like her father, Elizabeth faced numerous threats to her rule, including religious dissent and political plots. The Tower continued to serve as a prison for those who challenged the queen's authority, and it became the site of some of the most famous imprisonments of the Elizabethan era. One of the most notable prisoners during Elizabeth's reign was Robert Devereux, the Earl of Essex, a former favorite of the queen who fell out of favor and attempted to lead a rebellion against her. After his failed uprising, Essex was imprisoned in the Tower and ultimately executed in 1601. His downfall was a reminder of the precarious nature of power in the Tudor court and the Tower's role in enforcing royal authority.

Throughout the Tudor era, the Tower of London was not only a place of imprisonment and punishment but also a symbol of the monarchy's power and control. The fortress stood as a constant reminder of the consequences of opposing the Tudor monarchs, and its walls witnessed some of the most dramatic events in English history. The executions of high-profile figures such as Anne Boleyn, Thomas More, and the Earl of Essex were just a few of the many tragic events that unfolded within the Tower's walls during this period. The Tower's grim reputation as a place of death and despair was solidified during the Tudor era, and it became synonymous with the brutality and intrigue of the Tudor court.

In addition to its political and religious significance, the Tower also played a role in England's military and economic strategies during the Tudor era. As a royal fortress, the Tower was equipped to withstand sieges and attacks, and it housed a garrison of soldiers who were responsible for defending the city of London. The Tower's strategic location along the River Thames made it an important stronghold for protecting the capital from foreign invaders or domestic uprisings. The Tower also served as a royal mint, where coins were produced, and as a storage facility for arms and gunpowder, making it a critical center for the kingdom's military and economic operations.

In conclusion, the Tower of London during the Tudor era was a place of immense power, intrigue, and tragedy. It served as a royal residence, a political prison, and a symbol of the monarchy's authority. The Tower's walls bore witness to some of the most important events of the period, from the executions of queens and courtiers to the imprisonment of religious dissenters and political rivals. The Tudor monarchs used the Tower to consolidate their power, enforce their religious policies, and eliminate threats to their rule. The Tower's role during the Tudor era cemented its place in history as one of the most famous and feared structures in England, and its legacy as a site of political intrigue and royal power continues to captivate the imagination of those who visit it today.

Chapter 12: Escapes from the Tower of London

The Tower of London, with its towering walls, formidable defenses, and centuries-old reputation as an impenetrable fortress and prison, has long been associated with royal power, political intrigue, and death. For much of its nearly 1,000-year history, it served as a place of confinement for enemies of the Crown, from rebellious nobles and foreign dignitaries to religious dissenters and those who had fallen out of royal favor. The fortress was notorious for housing some of the most high-profile prisoners in English history. However, despite its fearsome reputation and secure construction, the Tower of London has also been the site of several daring and dramatic escapes. These escapes, though rare, have become legendary, capturing the imaginations of historians and storytellers alike. Over the centuries, the stories of those who managed to break free from the Tower's clutches have become part of its lore, and these escapes reflect the extraordinary determination, ingenuity, and courage of those involved.

One of the most famous escapes from the Tower of London took place in 1597 and involved John Gerard, a Jesuit priest imprisoned for his Catholic faith. In the Elizabethan era, Catholicism was considered treasonous, and priests like Gerard were hunted, captured, and imprisoned for defying the Protestant rule of Queen Elizabeth I. Gerard's story is one of remarkable courage and tenacity. He was imprisoned in the Tower's Salt Tower, where he was subjected to brutal torture in an attempt to force him to reveal information about other Catholics operating in England. Despite enduring extreme physical suffering, Gerard refused to betray his fellow Catholics. With the help of allies on the outside, he managed to escape in a daring and meticulously planned operation.

Gerard's escape began when he was smuggled a length of rope by one of his jailers, who had been bribed by his supporters. One dark night, Gerard made his way to the Tower's Cradle Tower, where the rope had been lowered from the riverbank by two fellow Jesuits. With his hands badly damaged from torture, Gerard had to wrap the rope around his wrists and use his arms to climb down the Tower's outer wall and over the moat. The physical effort was agonizing, but he eventually reached the riverbank and swam across the River Thames to safety. His escape from one of the most secure prisons in England was a stunning achievement, and Gerard would go on to write about his experiences in a memoir that detailed not only his escape but also his faith and defiance in the face of persecution. His story remains one of the most famous and extraordinary escapes from the Tower of London.

Another remarkable escape occurred in 1716 and involved Lord Nithsdale, a Scottish nobleman who had been imprisoned in the Tower for his role in the Jacobite Rising of 1715. The Jacobites were supporters of the deposed Catholic monarch, James II, and they sought to restore him and his descendants to the British throne. After the failed uprising, Lord Nithsdale was captured and sentenced to death. However, his wife, Lady Winifred Nithsdale, orchestrated an incredibly bold and creative plan to rescue him from certain execution. In what would become one of the most legendary escapes in British history, Lady Nithsdale disguised her husband as a woman and smuggled him out of the Tower.

The plan hinged on Lady Nithsdale's ability to fool the Tower's guards. On the night of the escape, she visited her husband in the Tower, bringing with her two female companions who were in on the plan. While one of the women distracted the guards, Lady Nithsdale dressed her husband in a woman's cloak, a wig, and a veil, effectively disguising him as one of her companions. The group then left the Tower together, with the guards none the wiser. Lord Nithsdale walked right out of his cell and out of the Tower without being recognized.

Once outside, he fled to France, where he lived in exile for the rest of his life. Lady Nithsdale's clever and courageous actions saved her husband from the executioner's block, and the story of their escape became a symbol of devotion, ingenuity, and defiance.

In 1722, another notable escape from the Tower took place when a man named William Maxwell, the Earl of Nithsdale, managed to break free. Maxwell was another Jacobite who had been imprisoned for his involvement in the Jacobite Rebellion. His escape was no less audacious than that of his predecessor, and it involved bribery and clever deception. Maxwell's supporters managed to bribe the Tower's guards, allowing him to slip out of his cell and escape under the cover of darkness. He was aided by his wife, who had visited him regularly during his imprisonment and had made the necessary arrangements for his escape. Like his fellow Jacobite Lord Nithsdale, Maxwell fled to the Continent, where he spent the rest of his life in exile. These escapes demonstrate how, even in the supposedly impregnable Tower of London, resourceful prisoners and their allies could exploit weaknesses in the fortress's defenses.

Perhaps one of the most daring and well-known escapes involved Ranulf Flambard, the Bishop of Durham, who became the first recorded prisoner to escape from the Tower of London in 1101. Flambard had been a key financial advisor to King William II, but after William's death, he was imprisoned in the Tower by the new king, Henry I, on charges of embezzlement. Unlike many of the later prisoners who would suffer within the Tower's walls, Flambard enjoyed a relatively comfortable imprisonment due to his high rank and wealth. He was able to bribe the guards and was allowed certain privileges, such as being provided with fine food and wine. It was this access to wine that ultimately led to his escape.

On the night of his escape, Flambard hosted a lavish banquet for his jailers, providing them with ample food and drink. Once the guards were sufficiently intoxicated, Flambard took advantage of their inebriation and made his move. A rope had been smuggled into his cell hidden in a wine cask, and Flambard used it to lower himself out of a window of the White Tower. Despite the considerable height and the danger of such a descent, Flambard successfully escaped from the Tower and fled to Normandy, where he joined forces with William the Conqueror's eldest son, Robert Curthose, who was then in rebellion against King Henry. Flambard's escape is often remembered as one of the earliest examples of the Tower's vulnerabilities, as even a fortress as imposing as the Tower could be breached by a combination of wit, bribery, and opportunity.

In 1746, during the aftermath of the Jacobite Rising of 1745, another dramatic escape took place, involving Charles Radclyffe, the 5th Earl of Derwentwater. Captured after the defeat of the Jacobites, Radclyffe was held in the Tower of London awaiting execution. Like many Jacobites before him, Radclyffe was sentenced to death for his role in the rebellion. However, his supporters devised a bold plan to help him escape. On the eve of his execution, Radclyffe's friends smuggled a disguise into the Tower, allowing him to dress as one of the many laborers working within the fortress. Disguised as a workman, Radclyffe managed to slip past the guards and leave the Tower unnoticed. Unfortunately, his freedom was short-lived, as he was eventually recaptured and executed. Nevertheless, his daring escape attempt is remembered as one of the many examples of Jacobite ingenuity and bravery in the face of overwhelming odds.

Escapes from the Tower of London were not limited to high-profile nobles and political figures. In some cases, ordinary criminals who were imprisoned in the Tower for various offenses also attempted—and sometimes succeeded—in breaking free. One such case occurred in 1661, when a man named Thomas Blood made an audacious attempt to steal the Crown Jewels, which were stored in the Tower. Blood, a notorious Irish adventurer, disguised himself as a parson and, with the help of accomplices, gained access to the Jewel House. His plan was to steal the Crown Jewels and escape undetected, but the plot was foiled when one of the Jewel House guards raised the alarm. Blood and his accomplices were captured, but his bold attempt to escape with the Crown Jewels became one of the most famous criminal escapades associated with the Tower of London. Remarkably, Blood was not executed for his crime; instead, he was pardoned by King Charles II, who was said to have been amused by the sheer audacity of the plan.

The Tower's reputation as an impenetrable fortress was further challenged by other minor escape attempts throughout its history. Some prisoners attempted to bribe their guards, while others sought to exploit weaknesses in the Tower's defenses, such as unsecured windows or poorly guarded gates. However, despite these occasional lapses in security, the Tower remained one of the most secure prisons in England for much of its history. Its thick stone walls, heavily armed guards, and numerous towers made it nearly impossible for most prisoners to escape without outside help.

While successful escapes from the Tower were rare, they became part of the fortress's mythos, adding to its reputation as a place of danger, intrigue, and high-stakes drama. The daring escapes of figures like John Gerard, Lord Nithsdale, and Ranulf Flambard demonstrated that even the most secure prison in the kingdom could be breached by those with the right combination of courage, cleverness, and outside support. These stories of escape have captured the imaginations of generations, serving as reminders that even in the darkest and most oppressive of circumstances, hope and resilience can lead to extraordinary acts of bravery.

In conclusion, the history of escapes from the Tower of London is filled with tales of ingenuity, courage, and audacity. From the earliest recorded escape by Ranulf Flambard to the daring efforts of Jacobites and religious dissenters, these stories reveal that even the most heavily fortified prisons are not immune to the resourcefulness of determined prisoners. Each escape, whether successful or not, contributed to the

Tower's rich and complex history as both a place of royal authority and a site of individual defiance. Today, the legends of these escapes continue to fascinate and inspire those who visit the Tower, reminding us that the human spirit's desire for freedom can sometimes triumph over even the most formidable of obstacles.

Chapter 13: The Royal Menagerie at the Tower

The Royal Menagerie at the Tower of London was one of the most fascinating and enduring institutions in the history of the Tower, serving as a home for exotic animals for more than 600 years. Established in the early medieval period, the menagerie became a symbol of royal power and prestige, as well as a source of curiosity and wonder for visitors. It showcased the wealth and global reach of the English monarchy, which was able to acquire rare and unusual creatures from far-off lands. Over time, the Royal Menagerie evolved from a private royal collection to a public attraction, and its story is intertwined with the history of the Tower itself, reflecting changes in royal power, imperial ambition, and attitudes toward animals and nature. The menagerie's history is filled with strange and often dramatic episodes involving the care, display, and sometimes dangerous interactions with the exotic animals that resided within the Tower's walls.

The origins of the Royal Menagerie can be traced back to the reign of King John in the early 13th century. Although records are sparse, it is believed that John, who ruled from 1199 to 1216, began collecting exotic animals as a symbol of his royal status. However, it was during the reign of his son, Henry III (1216-1272), that the menagerie became firmly established at the Tower of London. Henry III had a deep interest in animals and received several remarkable gifts from foreign rulers, which became the foundation of the Royal Menagerie. These animals, often seen as symbols of diplomacy and alliances between monarchs, were housed in the Tower's grounds, and their presence added to the grandeur and mystique of the fortress.

One of the earliest and most famous additions to the menagerie was a white bear, believed to be a polar bear, which was a gift from

King Haakon IV of Norway to Henry III in 1252. The bear was kept at the Tower, and according to contemporary accounts, it was allowed to swim and fish in the River Thames, tethered to a long chain. The sight of such an unusual creature swimming in the river must have been awe-inspiring to the people of London, who had likely never seen anything like it before. The polar bear quickly became one of the star attractions of the menagerie, symbolizing the monarch's power and connections to distant lands.

Another famous addition to the menagerie during Henry III's reign was an African elephant, presented to the king in 1255 by King Louis IX of France. The elephant, which was the first of its kind ever seen in England, was housed in a specially constructed wooden building at the Tower. Unfortunately, the elephant did not survive long in its new environment, as its keepers were unfamiliar with how to care for such a large and exotic animal. Contemporary accounts suggest that the elephant was fed a diet of meat and wine, which was unsuitable for the herbivorous creature, leading to its untimely death after only a few years. Despite the tragic fate of the elephant, its presence at the Tower helped solidify the menagerie's status as a unique and prestigious collection of animals.

As the menagerie grew over the centuries, it became home to an increasingly diverse array of creatures, many of which were gifts from foreign dignitaries. Lions, leopards, tigers, and other big cats became regular residents of the Tower, and they were often housed in cages within the Lion Tower, a special enclosure built specifically for them. The lions, in particular, became closely associated with the English monarchy, as the lion was a symbol of royal power and strength. At one point, there were so many lions at the Tower that they became a regular feature of royal ceremonies and pageantry, with their roars echoing through the fortress during important events. The Lion Tower became one of the most famous parts of the menagerie, and its animals were frequently mentioned in contemporary accounts of life at the Tower.

In addition to big cats, the menagerie also housed a wide variety of other exotic animals, including monkeys, baboons, camels, ostriches, and even a kangaroo. These animals, many of which came from Africa, Asia, and the New World, were seen as symbols of the British Empire's expanding reach and influence. The menagerie became a way for the monarchy to demonstrate its connections to the wider world and its ability to command the loyalty and tribute of foreign rulers. The animals were often presented as diplomatic gifts, and their presence at the Tower helped reinforce the image of the English monarchy as powerful and cosmopolitan.

The Royal Menagerie was not only a symbol of royal power but also a source of entertainment and education for the court and, later, the public. In the early years, the menagerie was a private collection, accessible only to the monarch and their guests. However, by the 16th century, access to the menagerie was gradually extended to members of the public, who could visit the Tower to see the exotic animals. For many ordinary people, a visit to the menagerie was a rare and exciting opportunity to glimpse creatures that they would never have seen otherwise. The menagerie became one of London's earliest tourist attractions, drawing visitors from across the city and beyond.

The animals of the menagerie were often treated as curiosities or spectacles, and their keepers were not always knowledgeable about their care. As a result, the animals sometimes lived in poor conditions, and there were several incidents in which visitors or even the keepers were attacked by the menagerie's inhabitants. In one famous case from the early 19th century, a keeper was mauled by a lion after mistakenly entering its cage. These dangers added to the menagerie's reputation as a place of excitement and unpredictability, where visitors could witness the raw power of the natural world up close.

By the 18th century, the menagerie had become an established part of life at the Tower, but it was also facing increasing criticism. Enlightenment thinkers, who were becoming more interested in the scientific study of animals and nature, began to question the ethics and practicality of keeping exotic animals in cramped enclosures in the heart of London. The menagerie's conditions were often harsh, with many animals suffering from poor nutrition, inadequate space, and the cold, damp climate. The animals' health and well-being were frequently compromised, and mortality rates were high. These concerns, combined with the growing interest in natural history and animal conservation, eventually led to calls for the closure of the Royal Menagerie.

In 1832, after centuries of housing exotic animals, the Royal Menagerie was finally closed by order of the Duke of Wellington, who was then the Constable of the Tower. The animals were transferred to the newly established London Zoo in Regent's Park, which had been founded by the Zoological Society of London in 1828. The zoo was seen as a more suitable environment for the care and study of exotic animals, and it provided larger, more natural enclosures for the animals to live in. The closure of the menagerie marked the end of an era for the Tower of London, but it also reflected changing attitudes toward the treatment of animals and the rise of modern zoological practices.

The legacy of the Royal Menagerie, however, lives on. Today, visitors to the Tower of London can still see traces of the menagerie's history, including sculptures of lions and other animals that once lived there. The Lion Tower, which was demolished in the 19th century, remains a site of historical interest, and its location is marked within the Tower complex. The stories of the menagerie's animals, from Henry III's polar bear to the lions of the Lion Tower, continue to capture the imagination of those who visit the Tower, and they provide a unique window into the history of royal power, imperial ambition, and the human fascination with the natural world.

The Royal Menagerie also holds a special place in the history of zoos and animal collections in Britain. It was one of the first royal menageries in Europe and set the precedent for other royal collections, such as those in Versailles and Vienna. The animals of the Tower inspired generations of artists, writers, and scientists, who used them as subjects for art, literature, and scientific study. The menagerie also played a role in the development of natural history in Britain, as it allowed scholars and naturalists to observe exotic animals up close and learn more about their behavior and biology. In this way, the Royal Menagerie contributed to the broader understanding of the natural world and the development of modern zoology.

In conclusion, the Royal Menagerie at the Tower of London was a remarkable and enduring institution that spanned more than six centuries. It was a symbol of royal power and prestige, a source of fascination and wonder for visitors, and a reflection of changing attitudes toward animals and nature. The menagerie's exotic inhabitants, from polar bears and lions to elephants and ostriches, represented the wealth and global reach of the English monarchy, while also providing entertainment and education to the public. Although the menagerie was eventually closed, its legacy lives on in the history of the Tower and in the modern institutions that have continued the work of studying and caring for animals. The story of the Royal Menagerie is a testament to the enduring human fascination with the natural world and the animals that inhabit it, as well as to the ways in which power, culture, and curiosity have shaped our relationship with the animal kingdom throughout history.

Chapter 14: The Tower's Role in World War II

The Tower of London, with its ancient walls steeped in history and a legacy stretching back nearly a thousand years, played a surprisingly active and symbolic role during World War II. As one of Britain's most iconic landmarks, the Tower had long been a symbol of royal power, authority, and national resilience. However, during the tumultuous years of the Second World War, its role shifted from that of a tourist attraction and historical monument to one of renewed military importance. It became a site of strategic defense, a prison for high-profile enemies of the state, a place for military executions, and even a target during the German bombing campaigns. The Tower's deep connection to Britain's past, combined with its active involvement in the war effort, makes its story during World War II both unique and poignant, as it became a living testament to Britain's endurance in the face of the greatest conflict the world had ever seen.

Before the outbreak of the war, the Tower of London had long been a place of history and tradition, with much of its military significance having faded into the background. However, as the war loomed closer in the late 1930s, the Tower's strategic value was reconsidered. Its location along the River Thames in central London and its fortified structure made it an ideal location for certain military activities. The British government recognized that every available space in London would need to be repurposed to support the war effort, and the Tower of London was no exception. Its large grounds, buildings, and storied past made it a suitable location for several vital wartime functions, including acting as a storage facility for important military equipment and as a headquarters for some military units.

One of the Tower's first roles during World War II was to serve as a secure location for the storage of ammunition and weapons. The

Tower had been used in this capacity before, particularly during earlier conflicts like the Napoleonic Wars, and its vast underground spaces and storerooms were well-suited for the safe keeping of munitions. As the British military prepared for the possibility of a German invasion, the Tower's armories were once again filled with guns, ammunition, and other military supplies, ready for use by London's defenders. The Tower's thick walls, moat, and secure position made it one of the safest locations for storing such materials during the early stages of the war, and it became an important part of London's defense infrastructure.

The Tower of London also played a key role in the defense of the capital itself. As London became a primary target for the German Luftwaffe during the Blitz, defensive positions were set up all over the city, including at the Tower. Anti-aircraft guns, searchlights, and observation posts were installed around the Tower grounds, with soldiers stationed there to defend against potential air raids. The Tower's strategic location along the Thames made it an important part of the city's air defense network. During the Blitz, London was bombed relentlessly by German aircraft, and these air defenses at the Tower helped to protect vital parts of the city, including government buildings, transportation hubs, and the nearby docks. The men stationed at the Tower were responsible for scanning the skies for enemy planes, coordinating with other air defense units, and firing upon the bombers as they approached.

During the Blitz, the Tower of London itself did not escape unscathed. German bombers frequently targeted central London, and the Tower's proximity to key areas like the docks and government buildings made it vulnerable to attack. In September 1940, the Tower was hit by several bombs during one of the Luftwaffe's raids. While the damage was significant, it was not catastrophic. Buildings within the Tower complex, such as the Royal Chapel of St. Peter ad Vincula, were damaged by the bombing, and parts of the Tower's famous walls were also affected. The White Tower, the oldest and most famous part of the complex, suffered some damage, though fortunately, it was not destroyed. Despite the damage caused by the bombing, the Tower's symbolic importance as a symbol of British resilience was only heightened. It stood as a reminder that even as the city was under attack, Britain's long history and enduring spirit could not be easily broken.

One of the most fascinating aspects of the Tower's role during World War II was its use as a prison for high-profile enemy combatants and spies. The Tower had a long history as a place of imprisonment for political prisoners, traitors, and enemies of the state, and during the war, this tradition was revived. Perhaps the most famous prisoner held at the Tower during World War II was Rudolf Hess, Adolf Hitler's deputy and one of the highest-ranking members of the Nazi regime. In May 1941, Hess made a bizarre solo flight to Scotland, where he attempted to broker peace between Nazi Germany and Britain. He was arrested upon his arrival and, due to the sensitive nature of his position within the Nazi hierarchy, was initially imprisoned in the Tower of London for his own safety. Hess was one of the last people to be held as a prisoner in the Tower, and his imprisonment there recalled the Tower's earlier role as a place of confinement for significant political figures. He was later transferred to other locations and eventually stood trial at Nuremberg after the war, but his brief imprisonment at the Tower was a reminder of the fortress's historical importance as a place of detention for enemies of the state.

In addition to Hess, several other individuals were imprisoned at the Tower during the war, many of whom were Nazi spies or collaborators captured by British intelligence. These prisoners were often held in secure cells within the Tower complex while they awaited trial or interrogation. The capture and imprisonment of enemy agents at the Tower highlighted Britain's determination to root out espionage and sabotage within its borders, and the Tower's reputation as a secure and imposing place of imprisonment made it a fitting location for such high-profile detainees. The presence of spies and enemy agents in the Tower during World War II was a reminder of the fortress's long history as a symbol of royal and national security.

Perhaps the most somber aspect of the Tower's role during World War II was its use as a site for military executions. While the Tower had not been used as a regular place of execution for many years, it was once again employed for this grim purpose during the war. Between 1941 and 1945, a number of German spies captured in Britain were tried, convicted, and executed within the Tower's walls. These executions were carried out in a small, secluded area of the Tower grounds known as the "Tower Green," which had been the site of famous executions in earlier centuries, including that of Anne Boleyn and Lady Jane Grey. During World War II, however, the executions were conducted in secret and with little fanfare, reflecting the seriousness of the war and the need to maintain morale and security in the face of enemy espionage.

One of the most notable executions carried out at the Tower during the war was that of Josef Jakobs, a German spy who was captured after parachuting into England in 1941. Jakobs had been sent to Britain on a mission to gather intelligence and sabotage military operations, but he was quickly apprehended by British authorities. After a military tribunal, Jakobs was sentenced to death for espionage, and he was executed by firing squad in the Tower's rifle range on August 15, 1941. Jakobs was the last person to be executed at the Tower of London, bringing an end to a long history of executions at the site that stretched back centuries. His execution marked the final chapter in the Tower's role as a place of death for those deemed enemies of the state.

Despite its military functions during the war, the Tower of London remained a symbol of British endurance and continuity. Even as the city around it was battered by bombs and air raids, the Tower stood as a reminder of Britain's long history of resilience in the face of adversity. The sight of the ancient fortress, still standing despite the destruction wrought by the Blitz, became a source of inspiration for Londoners and for the British people as a whole. The Tower, with its rich history of surviving invasions, rebellions, and sieges, seemed to embody the nation's determination to withstand the Nazi onslaught and continue fighting for freedom.

In the aftermath of the war, the Tower of London resumed its role as a tourist attraction and historical monument, but its involvement in World War II left a lasting mark on its history. The damage caused by the bombings was repaired, and the Tower's military functions were gradually wound down as peace returned to Britain. However, the memory of the Tower's wartime role, from the imprisonment of spies to its use as a defensive stronghold, remained an important part of its story. The Tower's connection to the war became part of the broader narrative of Britain's wartime experience, and it continued to serve as a powerful symbol of national resilience and continuity.

Today, visitors to the Tower of London can learn about its role in World War II through exhibits and displays that highlight the fortress's military significance during the conflict. The stories of the prisoners held there, the soldiers who defended it, and the bombs that fell upon it are all part of the Tower's rich and multifaceted history. The Tower's role during the war is a testament to its enduring importance as a symbol of British power, resilience, and determination, even in the face of one of the most devastating conflicts in human history. In many ways, the Tower of London's involvement in World War II was a continuation of its centuries-old role as a bastion of defense and a place where the fate of the nation was decided.

In conclusion, the Tower of London played a significant and multifaceted role during World War II, acting as a military stronghold, a prison for high-profile enemy agents, a site of executions, and a symbol of British resilience during the Blitz. Its history during the war is a reflection of both its strategic importance and its symbolic power, as it once again became a crucial part of Britain's defense against external threats. The Tower's ability to adapt to the demands of war, while still standing as a reminder of the nation's long and storied history, ensured that it remained relevant and meaningful even during one of the darkest periods in British history.

Chapter 15: The Bloody Tower's Dark Past

The Bloody Tower, one of the most infamous and haunting parts of the Tower of London, has long been associated with tales of murder, mystery, treachery, and dark deeds. Its name alone evokes a sense of foreboding and intrigue, a reflection of the many tragic and bloody events that have taken place within its walls over the centuries. Originally known as the Garden Tower, it acquired its grim moniker in the 16th century, thanks to the dark legends surrounding the disappearance of two young princes, whose mysterious deaths remain one of England's most notorious unsolved mysteries. However, the story of the Bloody Tower is not confined to this single tragedy. Its history is filled with a series of grim events, including imprisonments, political intrigue, and executions, all of which contribute to its reputation as one of the Tower of London's most sinister locations. The tower's dark past is a microcosm of the broader history of the Tower of London itself, a place where power struggles, royal ambition, and deadly betrayal played out over the centuries, leaving a legacy of blood and mystery that still captivates the imagination today.

The most famous and enduring story associated with the Bloody Tower is undoubtedly the tragic tale of the Princes in the Tower. This legend revolves around the mysterious disappearance and presumed murder of Edward V of England and his younger brother, Richard of Shrewsbury, Duke of York, who were only 12 and 9 years old, respectively. After the death of their father, King Edward IV, in 1483, young Edward V was set to inherit the throne. However, his uncle, Richard, Duke of Gloucester, later crowned as Richard III, took control of the government as the Lord Protector. Richard confined the two princes to the Tower of London, supposedly for their protection while Edward's coronation was being planned.

The princes were lodged in the Garden Tower, which later became known as the Bloody Tower, and it was here that they were last seen alive. In the months following their confinement, the young boys mysteriously vanished, and no clear explanation was given for their disappearance. It is widely believed that they were murdered to eliminate any challenge to Richard III's claim to the throne, but the exact circumstances of their deaths remain a subject of debate and speculation. Some historians believe that Richard III ordered their assassination, while others suggest that it may have been the work of the Duke of Buckingham or even Henry Tudor (later Henry VII), who also had a vested interest in removing rivals to the throne.

In 1674, workers carrying out renovations at the Tower of London uncovered a chest containing two small human skeletons buried beneath a staircase in the White Tower. These remains were widely believed to be those of the two princes, although this has never been definitively proven. The discovery only added to the macabre reputation of the Bloody Tower, and the mystery of the Princes in the Tower has continued to captivate people for centuries, with historians, writers, and even modern forensic experts attempting to unravel the truth behind their tragic fate. Regardless of who was responsible for their deaths, the princes' disappearance became one of the most infamous and enduring stories of royal intrigue and murder, casting a dark shadow over the Bloody Tower and the Tower of London as a whole.

The legend of the Princes in the Tower is just one of the many grim tales that have earned the Bloody Tower its sinister reputation. Over the centuries, the tower has been the site of numerous imprisonments, many of which ended in death or execution. During the turbulent reign of Queen Mary I (1553–1558), the Bloody Tower became the final home for several high-profile prisoners, many of whom were caught up in the religious and political upheavals of the time. Among these was Archbishop Thomas Cranmer, a leading figure of the English

Reformation, who was imprisoned in the Bloody Tower before being taken to Oxford to stand trial for heresy. Cranmer's imprisonment and subsequent execution by burning were part of Mary's efforts to restore Catholicism in England after the Protestant reforms initiated by her father, Henry VIII. The tower's walls bore silent witness to Cranmer's anguish as he awaited his fate, adding yet another layer of sorrow to its history.

Another notable prisoner held in the Bloody Tower was Sir Walter Raleigh, the famed English explorer, writer, and courtier, who spent a total of 13 years imprisoned there under James I. Raleigh's imprisonment was the result of his involvement in a plot to depose the king, known as the Main Plot, although his exact role in the conspiracy remains unclear. His first period of imprisonment began in 1603, shortly after the ascension of James I to the throne. While confined in the tower, Raleigh spent much of his time writing and conducting scientific experiments. During this time, he produced his famous *History of the World*, a monumental work that covered historical events from ancient times up to the Roman Empire. Despite the grim surroundings of the Bloody Tower, Raleigh managed to maintain his intellectual pursuits, turning his cell into a space of learning and reflection. However, in 1616, after being briefly released, Raleigh was imprisoned again, and this time his fate was sealed. He was executed in 1618, beheaded for treason, and his imprisonment in the Bloody Tower added to the tower's association with political intrigue, betrayal, and death.

The Bloody Tower also played a significant role in England's tumultuous relationship with religion during the 16th and 17th centuries. The Reformation and its aftermath saw the imprisonment of numerous religious figures, both Catholic and Protestant, who were caught up in the shifting tides of religious policy. Some were imprisoned for their beliefs, while others were accused of treasonous plots linked to their religious affiliations. One of the most famous of these prisoners was John Fisher, the Bishop of Rochester, who was imprisoned in the Bloody Tower for refusing to acknowledge Henry VIII's break with the Catholic Church and his declaration as Supreme Head of the Church of England. Fisher's principled stand ultimately cost him his life, and he was executed in 1535. The Bloody Tower, with its cold, oppressive atmosphere, became a place where religious martyrs and political prisoners alike awaited their deaths, their stories becoming woven into the dark tapestry of the Tower's history.

The association of the Bloody Tower with death and suffering is not limited to historical figures and events. Over the years, many ghost stories have arisen surrounding the tower, particularly involving the spirits of those who met their end within its walls. One of the most famous ghostly sightings is that of the two young princes. Many visitors and guards over the years have reported seeing the specters of two small boys dressed in 15th-century clothing, wandering the halls of the Bloody Tower. These apparitions are believed to be the restless spirits of Edward V and his brother, Richard, forever trapped in the place where they were last seen alive. The story of their ghostly appearances has become one of the most enduring and chilling tales associated with the Tower of London, adding a supernatural element to its already dark history.

In addition to the princes, the ghost of Sir Walter Raleigh is also said to haunt the Bloody Tower. Raleigh's long imprisonment and tragic end have left their mark on the tower's atmosphere, and some have reported seeing his ghostly figure pacing the halls or standing at a window, gazing out across the Tower grounds. Other ghostly sightings include the spirit of a woman, thought to be one of the many wives or mistresses of executed prisoners, who is said to wail and moan in the dead of night, her cries echoing through the stone corridors of the Bloody Tower.

Throughout the centuries, the Bloody Tower has been a place of imprisonment for not only the famous but also the forgotten, the ordinary individuals whose names have been lost to history but whose suffering contributed to the tower's notorious reputation. Political prisoners, religious dissenters, and common criminals were all held within its walls, often under harsh conditions. Many of these prisoners faced torture or execution, and their stories, though less well known, are part of the broader narrative of cruelty and injustice that defines the Bloody Tower's dark past. The tower's cells, once filled with the echoes of fear and despair, now serve as reminders of the brutality of the past and the precariousness of power in medieval and early modern England.

In modern times, the Bloody Tower continues to captivate visitors with its grim history. As part of the Tower of London's many exhibits, it stands as a testament to the darker side of British history, where political intrigue, royal ambition, and the clash of ideologies often ended in bloodshed. The tower's walls are steeped in the memory of the tragedies that occurred within, and the stories of the princes, Raleigh, and the many others who were imprisoned or killed there still resonate with those who visit today. The tower's enduring association with death, mystery, and the supernatural ensures that it remains one of the most compelling and eerie parts of the Tower of London, drawing countless visitors eager to explore its dark past.

In conclusion, the Bloody Tower's history is one of blood, betrayal, and tragedy. From the unsolved mystery of the Princes in the Tower to the imprisonments of Sir Walter Raleigh and Archbishop Thomas Cranmer, the tower's walls have witnessed some of the most dramatic and heartbreaking moments in British history. Its association with imprisonment, execution, and dark political intrigue has earned it a reputation as one of the most haunted and sinister places within the Tower of London. Whether through the legends of the ghosts that are said to haunt its halls or the chilling stories of those who suffered and died within its confines, the Bloody Tower remains a symbol of the darker side of power and ambition, where the pursuit of the crown could lead to death, and where history's forgotten voices still seem to echo through the cold stone corridors.

79

Chapter 16: The Tower as a Royal Residence

The Tower of London, perhaps best known for its role as a fortress, prison, and place of execution, also served an important function as a royal residence during various periods of English history. While its reputation today is largely associated with its darker past—imprisonments, intrigue, and treachery—it is easy to overlook the fact that the Tower was once a luxurious home for English monarchs. Over its centuries-long history, the Tower functioned as a royal palace, hosting kings, queens, and their courts. Its dual role as both a fortress and a royal residence underscores the Tower's importance not just as a symbol of military might but also as a center of royal power and governance.

The origins of the Tower of London as a royal residence date back to its construction by William the Conqueror after his victory at the Battle of Hastings in 1066. Following his conquest of England, William sought to establish his control over the newly acquired kingdom, and one of the key ways to do this was through the construction of a series of fortifications. The Tower of London was among the most significant of these, both because of its strategic location along the River Thames and because of its symbolic importance as a visible representation of Norman dominance over the Anglo-Saxon population. The White Tower, the original structure around which the rest of the complex would eventually grow, was not only a fortress but also a royal residence for William and his successors. As such, it was designed to serve both as a military stronghold and as a luxurious home fit for a king.

In the early years of its existence, the Tower of London played a crucial role in the monarch's ability to assert authority over the realm. When William the Conqueror was not traveling throughout his kingdom or campaigning on the continent, he would stay at the Tower. The White Tower served as a secure location for the king and his court, and its position at the heart of London made it an ideal residence from which to oversee governance and administration. While William's presence at the Tower was intermittent, subsequent monarchs would expand upon his initial design, making the Tower not only a center of military defense but also a lavish royal palace. Over the years, successive kings added to the Tower's layout, enhancing its grandeur and making it a more comfortable living space for themselves and their families.

One of the most significant additions to the Tower's role as a royal residence occurred during the reign of King Henry III, who ruled from 1216 to 1272. Henry III had a great love for architecture and was keen to enhance the royal palaces and castles of England. His reign saw the expansion of the Tower of London into a more elaborate royal residence. During this period, many of the buildings that would later become iconic parts of the Tower complex were constructed, including royal apartments, great halls, and chapels. These additions reflected Henry's desire to live in a palace that was not only secure but also befitting of his status as the ruler of England.

Henry III's enhancements to the Tower reflected his love of luxury and comfort. The royal apartments were richly decorated with tapestries, paintings, and fine furniture, and the king ensured that the Tower was furnished with all the necessities of a royal court. Special attention was given to the construction of a royal chapel within the Tower, known as the Chapel of St. Peter ad Vincula. This chapel would become the spiritual heart of the royal residence, where the monarch and his court could attend religious services. Under Henry's reign, the Tower became a place where governance and royal ceremony were conducted, as well as a home for the royal family.

Henry III's successor, Edward I, further strengthened the Tower's dual function as both a fortress and a royal residence. Edward, who ruled from 1272 to 1307, was a warlike king, known for his campaigns in Wales and Scotland, and he ensured that the Tower was fortified to withstand potential attacks. He reinforced the Tower's defenses with a series of new walls, moats, and towers, turning the Tower into a formidable military stronghold. Despite this focus on fortification, Edward I also understood the importance of the Tower as a royal residence, and like his predecessor, he made efforts to ensure that it remained a comfortable and luxurious home for the monarch.

The monarchs of England did not live in the Tower year-round, but they used it frequently for specific purposes. One of its key functions was as a secure location during times of unrest or conflict. Whenever the kingdom was threatened by rebellion or external invasion, the Tower became the monarch's primary residence due to its strong defensive capabilities. During times of internal strife, such as the Peasants' Revolt of 1381, kings and queens would retreat to the safety of the Tower, where they could be protected from potential uprisings. This dual role as both a home and a refuge reinforced the Tower's importance in the life of the English monarchy.

While the Tower served as a royal residence during times of unrest, it was also a ceremonial and symbolic home for the monarch during times of peace. Coronation processions often began at the Tower, with the newly crowned king or queen making a public journey from the fortress to Westminster Abbey. This ceremonial route, known as the Royal Procession, was an important display of royal authority, with the Tower representing the monarch's military power and Westminster symbolizing their religious and governmental authority. The Tower thus became an integral part of royal coronation traditions, and for many years, it served as the starting point for this important event.

Throughout the Middle Ages, the Tower remained an important royal residence, particularly during periods of political instability. One of the most infamous uses of the Tower as a royal home occurred during the Wars of the Roses, a series of conflicts between the rival houses of Lancaster and York for control of the English throne. During this turbulent period, the Tower was not only a residence for the reigning monarch but also a prison for those who fell out of favor. The Tower's role as a royal residence became intertwined with its darker function as a place of imprisonment and execution, as rival claimants to the throne were held within its walls and, in some cases, executed.

By the time of the Tudor dynasty, the Tower's role as a royal residence began to diminish, although it still played an important part in royal life. Henry VII, the first Tudor monarch, continued to use the Tower for ceremonial purposes, including his coronation procession. However, the Tudor monarchs began to favor other royal palaces, such as Hampton Court and the Palace of Whitehall, for their primary residences. Nonetheless, the Tower remained a key location for important royal events, including the imprisonment and execution of high-profile figures such as Anne Boleyn, Catherine Howard, and Lady Jane Grey, all of whom were former queens or claimants to the throne. These executions reinforced the Tower's reputation as a place of both royal splendor and brutal punishment.

One of the last significant uses of the Tower as a royal residence occurred during the reign of Elizabeth I. Following the death of her half-sister, Queen Mary I, Elizabeth was crowned queen in 1558, and like many monarchs before her, she used the Tower as part of her coronation ceremony. Before her coronation, Elizabeth spent several nights at the Tower, where she prepared for the public procession to Westminster Abbey. This tradition, which dated back centuries, linked the Tower to the sacred rite of coronation, symbolizing the monarch's authority and right to rule. However, after Elizabeth's reign, the Tower's use as a royal residence became increasingly rare, as newer and more comfortable palaces were built elsewhere in London.

By the time of the Stuart and Hanoverian monarchs in the 17th and 18th centuries, the Tower was no longer used as a royal residence. Its primary functions had shifted to that of a military garrison, a prison, and a storage site for armaments. However, the Tower continued to hold symbolic importance for the monarchy, particularly in its role as the home of the Crown Jewels. These priceless treasures, which are used during coronation ceremonies, have been housed in the Tower since the late 17th century, further linking the Tower to the monarchy, even though it was no longer the primary royal residence.

Despite the Tower's decline as a royal home, its legacy as a former residence of kings and queens remains an important part of its history. The royal apartments and halls that once housed monarchs and their courts are now key attractions for visitors, who come to see the lavish surroundings in which England's rulers once lived. The Tower's role as a royal residence offers a glimpse into a time when it was not only a place of military power but also a center of royal life, where governance, ceremony, and domestic life were intertwined.

In modern times, the Tower of London's role as a royal residence is largely symbolic, but it still retains its connection to the monarchy. The Tower remains a vital part of royal tradition, particularly through its role as the home of the Yeoman Warders, or Beefeaters, who act as ceremonial guards and guides for the Tower. The Crown Jewels, housed in the Jewel House, continue to be displayed to the public, and they play an essential role in royal coronations and other state ceremonies. While the days of kings and queens residing at the Tower are long gone, the building's connection to the monarchy is still strong, and its history as a royal residence continues to fascinate visitors from around the world.

In conclusion, the Tower of London's history as a royal residence is a testament to its importance as a center of royal power and governance. From its origins as a fortress built by William the Conqueror to its expansion under monarchs like Henry III and Edward I, the Tower served as both a military stronghold and a luxurious home for England's kings and queens. Though its use as a royal residence gradually diminished over the centuries, the Tower remains an iconic symbol of the British monarchy and its enduring connection to the history of England. The royal apartments and halls that once housed monarchs are now part of the Tower's rich historical legacy, offering a window into a time when the Tower was not only a place of imprisonment and execution but also a home for the ruling elite.

Chapter 17: The Tower as a Tourist Attraction Today

The Tower of London, once a symbol of royal power and military strength, has evolved into one of the most popular and historically rich tourist attractions in the world today. This iconic fortress, with its thousand-year history, draws millions of visitors annually from around the globe, offering a glimpse into England's medieval past, its royal traditions, and its darker chapters of intrigue, imprisonment, and execution. The Tower of London is not just an ancient structure of stone and iron—it is a living museum, housing relics of royalty, tales of the monarchy, and the shadowy mysteries that have shaped British history.

Visiting the Tower of London today is an immersive experience, offering far more than just a walk through history. The massive complex, with its imposing walls and varied buildings, invites visitors to explore every corner of its sprawling grounds, each with its own unique stories and significance. Visitors can step inside the White Tower, the original building commissioned by William the Conqueror after his victory in 1066, where they will find exhibits of medieval armor, weaponry, and the regal architecture that once sheltered England's monarchs. The White Tower houses the Royal Armouries collection, a stunning display of arms and armor dating back centuries, giving tourists a vivid picture of how warfare and defense played a crucial role in England's history. Henry VIII's famous armor, with its impressive size and elaborate decoration, is one of the most popular exhibits, drawing the attention of adults and children alike.

But the Tower of London is much more than a display of ancient arms and stone walls—it is a journey into the stories of real people who lived, ruled, or met their tragic ends within its shadowy halls. One of the main attractions is the Crown Jewels exhibit, where visitors can marvel at some of the most precious and priceless treasures of the British monarchy. The Crown Jewels, which include the coronation regalia used in royal ceremonies, such as crowns, scepters, orbs, and swords, are still used by the royal family today. Visitors are often in awe as they pass by the glittering gems, including the famous Koh-i-Noor diamond and the Imperial State Crown, adorned with thousands of precious stones. The exhibition offers a rare opportunity to witness firsthand the opulence and grandeur that have surrounded the British monarchy for centuries, and the Crown Jewels remain one of the top reasons why millions visit the Tower each year.

Another aspect of the Tower that continues to captivate tourists is its grim and often macabre history as a prison and place of execution. The Tower of London has witnessed the downfall of some of the most prominent figures in British history, including Anne Boleyn, Catherine Howard, and Lady Jane Grey, all of whom met their untimely deaths at the scaffold. As visitors walk through Traitors' Gate, the infamous entrance through which prisoners were brought by boat on the River Thames, they can feel the weight of history, imagining the fear and dread that must have filled those about to face trial or execution. The Bloody Tower, long associated with the tragic disappearance and presumed murder of the young Princes in the Tower, Edward V and his brother Richard, Duke of York, remains one of the most chilling locations. The tower's haunted reputation and the mystery surrounding the fate of the princes continue to intrigue visitors, making it a must-see on any tour of the complex.

Guided tours led by the Yeoman Warders, popularly known as Beefeaters, are one of the highlights of a visit to the Tower. These ceremonial guards, who have served as the keepers of the Tower for centuries, not only protect the site but also bring its history to life with their detailed and often humorous commentary. Their tours are filled with anecdotes, legends, and lesser-known facts, giving visitors a personal connection to the Tower's many layers of history. The

Beefeaters themselves are a symbol of the Tower, dressed in their iconic uniforms and embodying the long-standing traditions of service to the Crown. For many tourists, interacting with the Beefeaters is a memorable part of the visit, adding a human touch to the otherwise daunting fortress.

The Tower's execution site, marked by a simple memorial, is another poignant spot that draws visitors' attention. Situated on Tower Green, this is where many high-profile figures, including two of Henry VIII's wives, Anne Boleyn and Catherine Howard, were beheaded. The site is marked by a small glass sculpture that commemorates those who lost their lives in the Tower. The memorial, with its simple yet evocative design, encourages visitors to reflect on the brutal history that took place within these walls. It is a reminder that, for all its grandeur and royal connections, the Tower was also a place of immense suffering and injustice. The execution site stands as a powerful symbol of the darker side of England's past.

The Tower also houses the Medieval Palace, where visitors can step back in time and experience what life was like for kings and queens in the Middle Ages. This area of the Tower has been carefully reconstructed to showcase the lavish living quarters of monarchs such as Henry III and Edward I. Visitors can see how these rulers lived in luxury, with richly decorated chambers, elaborate furniture, and tapestries that reflected their wealth and power. This part of the Tower helps to round out the visitor experience, offering not just a glimpse into the Tower's military and political history, but also into the domestic lives of the royal family.

In addition to its historical significance, the Tower of London has also embraced its role as a site for educational programs and events. Throughout the year, the Tower hosts a variety of themed events, including reenactments of historical battles, medieval festivals, and educational workshops. These activities are designed to engage visitors of all ages, particularly families and school groups, making the Tower not only a place of historical interest but also an interactive learning experience. For children, the Tower offers special family-friendly activities, including treasure hunts, interactive exhibits, and storytelling sessions that bring history to life in a fun and engaging way. The combination of history, legend, and interactive experiences makes the Tower a popular destination for families, ensuring that younger visitors are just as captivated as their parents.

Ghost stories and supernatural legends are another major draw for visitors. Over the centuries, the Tower has been the subject of numerous ghost sightings and paranormal tales. Many believe that the Tower is haunted by the spirits of those who met their deaths within its walls, with the ghosts of Anne Boleyn and the Princes in the Tower being among the most famous. For those intrigued by the Tower's eerie reputation, nighttime tours offer a chance to explore the grounds after dark, when the fortress takes on a more mysterious and foreboding atmosphere. These ghost tours, led by expert guides, delve into the Tower's haunted past and explore the various legends and ghostly encounters that have been reported over the years. They are particularly popular during Halloween, when the Tower's dark and unsettling history seems even more palpable.

The Tower of London's role as a modern tourist attraction is also supported by its UNESCO World Heritage status, a designation that highlights its global cultural and historical importance. As one of the most well-preserved medieval fortresses in the world, the Tower stands as a testament to the enduring legacy of British history, architecture, and tradition. This designation helps to protect the Tower and ensures that it will remain a cherished part of the global cultural heritage for future generations. Visitors come not only to learn about British history but also to appreciate the architectural marvel that the Tower represents. Its impressive construction, with its combination of Norman, medieval, and later additions, provides a unique opportunity to study the evolution of fortress architecture over the centuries.

In addition to its historical and cultural significance, the Tower plays an important role in contemporary royal events. The Tower continues to serve as a backdrop for royal ceremonies, such as the annual Ceremony of the Keys, a tradition that dates back over 700 years. Every evening, this ancient ceremony takes place, in which the Tower is securely locked and the keys are delivered to the monarch's representative. Visitors can witness this ritual as part of special tours, offering a rare opportunity to see a piece of living history in action. The Ceremony of the Keys is a reminder that, while the Tower is now primarily a tourist attraction, it still retains its connection to the British Crown and its traditions.

Moreover, the Tower's role as the home of the Yeoman Warders and the Royal Fusiliers adds a modern dimension to its historic significance. The Yeoman Warders, who live within the Tower grounds, continue their centuries-old duties of guarding the fortress and its treasures, while the Royal Fusiliers, a regiment of the British Army, maintain a presence within the Tower, reinforcing its role as a living military site. The Tower's function as both a historical monument and an active part of British military and royal life ensures that it remains a dynamic and relevant part of modern Britain, even as it draws tourists from around the world.

In conclusion, the Tower of London's transformation from a medieval fortress, royal palace, and prison into one of the world's most popular tourist attractions reflects its enduring significance in British history. Visitors today are drawn by its rich and varied past, its royal connections, its dark tales of imprisonment and execution, and its priceless treasures. Whether exploring the White Tower's ancient halls, gazing at the glittering Crown Jewels, or hearing the stories of famous prisoners and ghostly legends, a visit to the Tower is an immersive experience that brings history to life. Its blend of educational programs, interactive exhibits, and historical reenactments ensures that it remains a captivating destination for all ages. Even in the modern era, the Tower of London stands as a symbol of British heritage, attracting millions of visitors eager to walk in the footsteps of kings, queens, and prisoners who once called this iconic fortress home.

91

Chapter 18: Treasures and Secrets Hidden in the Tower

The Tower of London is renowned not only for its iconic architecture and rich history but also for the many treasures and secrets it has guarded for over a millennium. As one of the most secure fortresses in England, the Tower has been a place where monarchs, nobles, and even enemies of the state have hidden or protected their most valuable possessions. Its walls have safeguarded the Crown Jewels, rare artifacts, and untold wealth, while its darkened corridors have whispered rumors of secret chambers, tunnels, and buried fortunes. Over the centuries, the Tower has become synonymous with intrigue, mystery, and concealed treasures—some of which remain shrouded in legend even today.

Perhaps the most famous treasures housed within the Tower of London are the Crown Jewels, a glittering collection of regalia used during royal coronation ceremonies, state occasions, and important public events. These priceless treasures have been stored at the Tower since 1661, following the restoration of the monarchy under King Charles II. The collection includes some of the most iconic symbols of the British monarchy, such as the Imperial State Crown, the Sovereign's Orb, and the Sovereign's Sceptre, which are still in use today. The jewels are not merely ornamental; each piece holds deep symbolic significance, representing the monarch's authority, power, and divine right to rule.

At the heart of this collection lies the Imperial State Crown, one of the most recognizable crowns in the world. Adorned with thousands of diamonds, sapphires, emeralds, and rubies, the crown includes some of the most famous gems in history. Among them is the Cullinan II diamond, also known as the Second Star of Africa, a 317-carat diamond that was cut from the largest gem-quality diamond ever found. The Cullinan Diamond was discovered in South Africa in 1905 and presented to King Edward VII. The Imperial State Crown also contains St. Edward's Sapphire, believed to have belonged to Edward the Confessor, one of the last Anglo-Saxon kings of England. This sapphire is set in the cross at the top of the crown and adds to its aura of ancient royalty.

Another dazzling piece in the Crown Jewels is the Sovereign's Sceptre, which features the Cullinan I diamond, also known as the Great Star of Africa. Weighing an astonishing 530 carats, it is the largest clear-cut diamond in the world and symbolizes the monarch's temporal power and authority. The Sovereign's Orb, meanwhile, is a golden globe encrusted with precious jewels and topped with a cross, symbolizing the Christian world and the monarch's role as God's representative on Earth. These treasures, housed in the Jewel House within the Tower, are viewed by millions of visitors every year, who come to witness the glittering symbols of Britain's monarchy up close. The Crown Jewels, however, are more than just an exhibit—they remain an integral part of the royal tradition, with many items still used in coronations and royal ceremonies.

The history of the Crown Jewels is not without its drama and intrigue. In 1671, the Tower was the site of one of the most infamous heist attempts in British history. Colonel Thomas Blood, a notorious Irish adventurer, made a daring attempt to steal the Crown Jewels. Disguised as a parson, Blood and his accomplices managed to overpower the Jewel House keeper and seize several pieces, including the royal crown and sceptre. However, as they tried to make their escape, Blood was captured, and the jewels were recovered. Remarkably, despite his brazen crime, Blood was pardoned by King Charles II and even given a pension. The reasons for this royal leniency remain a mystery, adding yet another layer of intrigue to the Tower's history.

Beyond the Crown Jewels, the Tower has housed countless other treasures over the centuries, some of which are more hidden and less known to the public. One of the Tower's lesser-known but fascinating features is its role as a secure storage site for vast amounts of wealth during times of war and national crisis. Throughout history, during periods of political unrest, the Tower has served as a depository for both the monarch's personal wealth and the national treasury. During the reign of Henry VIII, for instance, the Tower housed an enormous amount of gold and silver, much of it seized from monasteries during the Dissolution of the Monasteries. This vast treasure trove was vital to Henry's military campaigns and the consolidation of his power.

In addition to its role as a storehouse for royal wealth, the Tower has also played a key role in the minting and safeguarding of currency. For over 500 years, from the 13th century to the 19th century, the Royal Mint operated within the Tower's walls. The Mint produced the coins that circulated throughout the kingdom, and the Tower was considered one of the most secure places to store precious metals, particularly silver and gold. The Royal Mint's presence at the Tower added another layer of significance to the fortress, making it not just a military stronghold but also a financial hub. Today, visitors can explore the history of the Royal Mint in one of the Tower's many exhibits, learning about the intricate process of coin production and the Mint's role in shaping the economy of medieval and early modern England.

Beyond these tangible treasures, the Tower has long been associated with hidden wealth and secret chambers, some of which are the subject of enduring legends and folklore. One of the most famous legends associated with the Tower is that of buried treasure, particularly that of King John's lost treasure. According to legend, King John, infamous for his role in the Magna Carta crisis, lost a vast hoard of treasure in the Wash, a tidal estuary in eastern England, during his retreat from rebellious barons. While much of this treasure was never recovered, rumors persist that some of it may have been hidden within the Tower of London. To this day, treasure hunters and historians alike are intrigued by the possibility that valuable items from King John's lost fortune may be concealed somewhere within the Tower's walls or underground chambers.

The Tower's subterranean world adds another layer of mystery to the fortress's history. Secret tunnels are said to run beneath the Tower, connecting it to other key locations in London, such as the Palace of Westminster. While some of these tunnels are real, having been used by monarchs and military leaders for escape or covert movement, others are the stuff of legend. Stories abound of hidden passages leading to treasure chambers deep beneath the Tower, accessible only to those with knowledge of their location. While the existence of such treasure chambers remains unproven, the allure of secret tunnels has captured the imaginations of many who visit the Tower, eager to uncover its hidden depths.

Another fascinating but lesser-known treasure once housed in the Tower was the Royal Menagerie, a collection of exotic animals gifted to the English monarchy by foreign rulers. These animals, including lions, tigers, elephants, and polar bears, were kept within the Tower as a symbol of the monarch's power and reach across the globe. While the animals were not treasures in the traditional sense, they were considered valuable gifts that reflected the wealth and influence of the English Crown. The Royal Menagerie, which existed from the 13th century until the 19th century, became one of the Tower's most popular attractions in its time, and remnants of its history are still visible today. Visitors can learn about the menagerie through exhibits that showcase the exotic animals once housed in the Tower and the role they played in royal diplomacy and entertainment.

In addition to material treasures, the Tower of London has been the repository of invaluable historical secrets. Over the centuries, the Tower has been the site of numerous plots, conspiracies, and clandestine meetings. Some of the kingdom's most sensitive state secrets have been kept within its walls. During the reign of Elizabeth I, for instance, the Tower was home to many of the documents and intelligence reports gathered by her spymaster, Sir Francis Walsingham. The Tower became a focal point for the Elizabethan government's efforts to thwart Catholic plots against the Protestant queen, and many of the prisoners held within the Tower during this period were involved in treasonous conspiracies. The Tower's role as a center of intelligence and espionage continues to fascinate historians, who have unearthed countless documents and letters that reveal the complex web of intrigue that surrounded the Elizabethan court.

The Tower's dark history as a place of imprisonment and execution also adds to its aura of secrets and mystery. Many of the Tower's prisoners, especially those accused of treason, were believed to have hidden important information or secrets that they took to their graves. The fate of the two young princes, Edward V and his brother Richard, Duke of York, remains one of the Tower's most enduring mysteries. Known as the Princes in the Tower, they disappeared while under the protection of their uncle, Richard III, and their ultimate fate has never been conclusively determined. Some believe that their bodies are buried somewhere within the Tower grounds, and while skeletal remains have been discovered in the Tower's walls and beneath its floors, the mystery of the princes' disappearance continues to fuel speculation about the Tower's hidden secrets.

The Tower of London, with its vast history of wealth, power, and intrigue, remains a treasure trove in more ways than one. Whether it's the priceless Crown Jewels, the lost fortunes of kings, or the many secrets whispered within its ancient walls, the Tower continues to captivate the imagination of those who visit. Its blend of tangible treasures, hidden mysteries, and centuries-old legends ensures that the Tower will remain a symbol of British history's richness and complexity for generations to come.

Chapter 19: The Tower Bridge and Its Connection

Tower Bridge is one of the most iconic landmarks in London, a masterpiece of Victorian engineering and a symbol of the city's grandeur and innovation. Spanning the River Thames, this remarkable bascule and suspension bridge connects the northern and southern parts of the city, close to the historic Tower of London, from which it takes its name. While often confused with London Bridge, Tower Bridge stands as a distinct structure, admired for its two majestic towers, intricate machinery, and picturesque views of London. Since its completion in 1894, Tower Bridge has not only played a crucial role in the city's transportation system but has also become a beloved tourist attraction and a key element of London's skyline. Its connection to the Tower of London and its place in the heart of the capital's history make it a vital part of the city's identity, bridging the past and present, both literally and metaphorically.

The need for Tower Bridge arose in the late 19th century, during a time when London was undergoing rapid expansion due to industrialization and population growth. The East End of London, in particular, was booming, with ships crowding the Thames and the docks handling vast amounts of cargo from Britain's global empire. London Bridge, which had been the main crossing point over the Thames for centuries, was struggling to cope with the increasing traffic. A new bridge was needed to alleviate the congestion and provide another crucial connection across the river. However, there was a significant challenge: the new bridge had to accommodate the needs of shipping traffic as well as road traffic. The design of Tower Bridge needed to allow large ships to pass through while providing a permanent crossing for vehicles and pedestrians.

In 1876, a special committee was formed to find a solution. After much debate and many different proposals, the winning design came from architect Sir Horace Jones, who was also the City of London's surveyor, and engineer Sir John Wolfe Barry. Together, they created a hybrid structure combining a bascule bridge, which could open to allow ships to pass, with a suspension bridge that would provide support for the roadway. This innovative design was both practical and aesthetically striking, with its two towers rising above the river, connected by high-level walkways that offered a unique perspective of the city. The Victorian Gothic style of the towers, with their pointed arches and intricate detailing, was chosen to complement the nearby Tower of London, creating a visual harmony between the old fortress and the new bridge.

Construction of Tower Bridge began in 1886 and took eight years to complete. Over 11,000 tons of steel were used to form the framework of the towers and walkways, which were then clad in Cornish granite and Portland stone to give the bridge its distinctive appearance. The use of steel was a cutting-edge choice at the time, showcasing the industrial might of Britain during the height of the Victorian era. The construction process was a monumental effort, involving hundreds of workers and the excavation of massive foundations on both sides of the river. The towers themselves were built on piers sunk deep into the riverbed, providing the necessary stability for the immense weight of the structure.

One of the most remarkable features of Tower Bridge is its bascule mechanism, which allows the central section of the bridge to be raised and lowered to let ships pass through. The word "bascule" comes from the French term for "see-saw," and the design uses enormous counterweights to balance the two halves, or leaves, of the bridge as they rise. Originally, the bascules were powered by steam engines, which were state-of-the-art technology at the time. The engines operated a complex system of hydraulics that could lift the 1,000-ton bascules in just a few minutes, allowing even the largest ships to pass. The opening of the bridge is an awe-inspiring sight, with the two halves rising up to create a wide passage for river traffic. Today, the bascules are operated by electric motors, but the original steam engines and hydraulic machinery are still on display in the bridge's engine rooms, offering visitors a glimpse into the engineering marvels of the past.

In addition to its functional role, Tower Bridge quickly became a symbol of London's industrial prowess and architectural innovation. Its combination of form and function—balancing the needs of river and road traffic while maintaining an elegant and imposing presence—was widely praised. The high-level walkways, originally intended for pedestrians to use while the bridge was raised, offered spectacular views of the Thames and the city, though in the early years, they were not very popular and were eventually closed. Today, however, the walkways have been reopened as part of the Tower Bridge Exhibition, a popular attraction that allows visitors to walk across the glass-floored paths and enjoy panoramic views of London from 42 meters above the river.

Tower Bridge's connection to the Tower of London is more than just geographical. Both structures symbolize different aspects of London's rich history—one representing its medieval past and the other its industrial future. The proximity of the two landmarks creates a powerful juxtaposition of old and new, reminding visitors of the city's ability to evolve while preserving its heritage. The Tower of London, with its centuries of history as a royal palace, prison, and fortress, sits just a short distance from the modern engineering marvel of Tower Bridge. This physical closeness reflects London's layered history, where different eras coexist side by side. The bridge was deliberately designed to complement the Tower, ensuring that the new structure would not overshadow the ancient fortress but instead enhance its grandeur.

Over the years, Tower Bridge has witnessed countless significant events in London's history. It has been part of royal processions, state occasions, and public celebrations. During Queen Elizabeth II's

Diamond Jubilee in 2012, Tower Bridge was a centerpiece of the river pageant, where over a thousand boats sailed down the Thames in honor of the Queen's 60-year reign. The bridge was decorated with the royal coat of arms and flags, serving as a striking backdrop to the festivities. In 2015, the bridge played a key role in the celebrations marking the 800th anniversary of the Magna Carta, with a grand flotilla of boats passing underneath in a symbolic reenactment of the historical significance of the River Thames to British history.

Throughout the 20th and 21st centuries, Tower Bridge has remained a vital part of London's transportation infrastructure. Despite its historical significance, the bridge continues to serve its original purpose as a working bascule bridge, opening regularly to allow river traffic to pass through. Ships, including large cruise liners, naval vessels, and historical ships, still navigate the Thames, and Tower Bridge opens around 800 times a year to accommodate them. The bridge's ability to maintain its practical function while becoming a beloved tourist attraction speaks to its enduring design and importance.

In recent years, Tower Bridge has become a focal point for public art, events, and light displays, further cementing its place as a symbol of modern London. The bridge is often illuminated in different colors to mark special occasions, such as national holidays, royal anniversaries, and international events. During the 2012 London Olympics, Tower Bridge was famously lit up with the Olympic rings, providing a dramatic backdrop for the games and showcasing London's role as a global city. The bridge's lighting system, which has been upgraded in recent years to use energy-efficient LED lights, allows for dynamic displays that can change color and pattern, turning the bridge into a canvas for artistic expression.

The Tower Bridge Exhibition, opened in 1982, offers visitors a chance to explore the history and mechanics of the bridge in detail. The exhibition includes access to the high-level walkways, the Victorian engine rooms, and interactive displays that explain the bridge's construction, its role in London's history, and the technology that powers its bascules. Visitors can also see the original control rooms and learn about the men and women who worked to keep the bridge operating smoothly throughout its history. One of the highlights of the exhibition is the glass floor installed in the walkways in 2014, allowing visitors to look down and see the traffic and river passing beneath their feet—a thrilling experience for those not afraid of heights.

Tower Bridge's status as a tourist attraction does not detract from its role as a functional piece of infrastructure. It continues to handle road traffic across the Thames, with thousands of vehicles and pedestrians crossing it every day. The bridge's ability to blend its historical significance with its modern utility makes it a unique part of London's landscape. Whether viewed from the riverbanks, walked across by tourists, or sailed beneath by ships, Tower Bridge remains a vital connection within the city, linking the ancient and modern parts of London in a way that few other landmarks can.

In conclusion, Tower Bridge is much more than a simple crossing over the River Thames; it is a symbol of London's history, engineering brilliance, and ability to balance tradition with innovation. Its connection to the Tower of London reinforces its place within the fabric of the city's history, representing both the medieval past and the industrial progress of the 19th century. Tower Bridge's enduring appeal, both as a functional bridge and a beloved tourist attraction, ensures that it will continue to be a central part of London's identity for generations to come. Its towering presence over the Thames, its intricate design, and its blend of utility and beauty make it one of the most remarkable and enduring symbols of the city.

Chapter 20: The Tower Through the Centuries

The Tower of London, one of Britain's most iconic landmarks, has stood as a silent witness to nearly a thousand years of history, its thick walls and formidable towers guarding secrets, treasures, and tales of power and intrigue. From its earliest beginnings as a symbol of Norman dominance to its evolving role in the modern age, the Tower has been a fortress, palace, prison, treasury, and even a menagerie. Its story is a reflection of the changing times, the rise and fall of monarchs, the ebb and flow of power, and the transformation of England from a medieval kingdom to a modern global power. The Tower through the centuries is a narrative of resilience, adaptation, and endurance—a living monument that has both shaped and been shaped by the history of England.

The Tower's origins date back to the Norman Conquest of 1066, when William the Conqueror, having defeated King Harold at the Battle of Hastings, sought to consolidate his hold over England. The construction of the Tower began around 1078, part of a network of fortresses that William built to secure his new kingdom and assert Norman authority over the Saxon population. The Tower's location on the eastern edge of the City of London was strategically chosen to control the Thames, the vital artery of trade and communication, and to dominate the city itself, which was the economic heart of England. At its core stood the White Tower, a massive stone keep that was both a defensive stronghold and a symbol of the king's power. The White Tower, with its thick walls and imposing structure, was designed to withstand attacks and serve as a residence for the monarch.

Throughout the 12th and 13th centuries, the Tower of London expanded under successive kings. Henry III, who reigned from 1216 to 1272, was particularly responsible for transforming the Tower from a simple fortress into a royal palace. He added new buildings, improved the defensive walls, and created a more comfortable living space for the royal family. It was during this period that the Tower became a true royal residence, with lavish apartments, great halls, and chapels. Henry's son, Edward I, continued his father's work, adding the outer curtain wall, a moat, and further fortifications. By the end of the 13th century, the Tower had become one of the most secure and formidable castles in Europe, with multiple layers of defenses designed to repel even the most determined attackers.

As the Middle Ages progressed, the Tower's role as a military stronghold was complemented by its growing significance as a political and administrative center. The Tower became the site of the royal mint, where coins were produced, and it housed the treasury, where the wealth of the kingdom was stored. It also became a prison for important political prisoners, many of whom were held in the Tower under harsh conditions. Some of the Tower's most famous inmates included William Wallace, the Scottish hero; John Balliol, the deposed King of Scotland; and later, during the Wars of the Roses, key figures from both the Yorkist and Lancastrian factions. The Tower's role as a prison grew over time, and its reputation as a place of terror and despair was cemented by the executions that took place there, particularly on Tower Green, where high-profile prisoners such as Anne Boleyn and Lady Jane Grey were beheaded.

During the Tudor era, the Tower reached the height of its notoriety as a prison. Henry VIII, famous for his six wives and his break with the Catholic Church, used the Tower to imprison and execute those who stood in his way, including two of his queens, Anne Boleyn and Catherine Howard. The Tower also played a key role in the political turmoil of the Reformation, when religious dissenters, both Catholic and Protestant, were imprisoned and executed for their beliefs. The Tower's bloody history continued under Henry's children, Edward VI, Mary I, and Elizabeth I. Mary, known as "Bloody Mary" for her persecution of Protestants, imprisoned her half-sister Elizabeth in the Tower, suspecting her of involvement in plots to overthrow her. Elizabeth's eventual release and accession to the throne in 1558 marked a turning point in the Tower's history, as her reign ushered in a period of relative stability and prosperity for England.

As England transitioned from the medieval to the early modern period, the Tower's role began to change. While it continued to be used as a prison, particularly for political prisoners and high-ranking individuals, it was no longer the primary royal residence. The Tudor monarchs, and later the Stuarts, preferred to live in more comfortable and modern palaces such as Hampton Court and the Palace of Whitehall. The Tower's military importance also diminished as advances in artillery made its medieval defenses less effective against modern warfare. However, the Tower remained an important symbol of royal authority and continued to house the Crown Jewels, the royal armory, and the state archives.

One of the most dramatic events in the Tower's history occurred in 1649, during the English Civil War, when King Charles I was executed and the monarchy was temporarily abolished. Under the rule of Oliver Cromwell and the Commonwealth, the Tower of London fell into disrepair, and many of its treasures were sold off or melted down, including much of the medieval regalia. However, when the monarchy was restored in 1660 with the coronation of Charles II, the Tower regained its status as a symbol of royal power. New Crown Jewels were created, and the Tower once again became a place of ceremonial importance, particularly during coronations and other state occasions.

The 18th century saw the Tower of London's role continue to evolve. Although it was no longer a primary royal residence or fortress, it remained an important military installation and administrative center. The Royal Mint operated within the Tower until 1810, producing coins that were circulated throughout the kingdom. The Tower also served as a military depot, storing weapons, ammunition, and supplies. However, its role as a prison began to decline. By the early 19th century, the Tower was used primarily for the imprisonment of political and military prisoners, many of whom were held there during the Napoleonic Wars. The Tower's last state prisoner was Rudolf Hess, Adolf Hitler's deputy, who was briefly held there during World War II.

The Tower's transformation into a tourist attraction began in the 19th century, as public interest in the history and legends surrounding the Tower grew. Queen Victoria's reign saw a renewed interest in the medieval past, and the Tower of London, with its dark history of imprisonment, torture, and execution, became a popular destination for visitors. The Tower was opened to the public in the mid-19th century, and new exhibitions were created to showcase the Crown Jewels, the Royal Armories, and other treasures housed within its walls. The Tower's role as a symbol of British history and heritage was solidified during this period, as it became a place where visitors could experience the drama and grandeur of England's past.

The 20th century brought further changes to the Tower of London. During World War I, it was used to hold German prisoners of war, and several spies were executed within its walls. In World War II, the Tower was again used for military purposes, with the moat being turned into an air-raid shelter and the buildings being used for various war-related activities. The last execution at the Tower took place in 1941, when Josef Jakobs, a German spy, was shot by a firing squad. After the war, the Tower resumed its role as a tourist attraction, and extensive restoration work was carried out to preserve its historic structures.

Today, the Tower of London is one of the most visited tourist sites in the United Kingdom, attracting millions of visitors each year. Its status as a UNESCO World Heritage Site underscores its historical and cultural significance, and it continues to play a role in British ceremonial life. The Crown Jewels, housed in the Jewel House, remain a major draw for visitors, as does the Tower's long and often gruesome history. The Beefeaters, or Yeoman Warders, who once guarded the

Tower and its prisoners, now serve as guides, leading tours and sharing the stories and legends that have made the Tower famous.

The Tower's enduring appeal lies in its ability to adapt to the changing needs of the monarchy and the nation while preserving its connection to the past. Over the centuries, it has been a fortress, a palace, a prison, a place of execution, and a site of national treasure. It has housed kings and queens, traitors and spies, soldiers and prisoners. It has witnessed the rise and fall of dynasties, the execution of queens, and the plotting of revolutions. Through it all, the Tower has remained a symbol of power, authority, and endurance.

In many ways, the Tower of London is a microcosm of English history. Its story mirrors the broader changes that have shaped the nation, from the Norman Conquest to the present day. The Tower has witnessed the growth of England from a feudal kingdom to a global empire, from a place of absolute monarchy to a constitutional state. Its walls have seen triumphs and tragedies, glory and suffering, power and punishment. Yet through the centuries, the Tower has stood firm, a silent sentinel watching over the Thames, guarding the treasures and secrets of a nation that has itself changed dramatically over time.

In conclusion, the Tower of London is not merely a relic of the past, but a living monument that continues to capture the imagination of people around the world. It is a place where history comes alive, where the stories of kings, queens, prisoners, and soldiers blend together in a tapestry that stretches back nearly a thousand years. From its early days as a Norman fortress to its current status as a world-renowned tourist attraction, the Tower has played a central role in the history of England. It is a testament to the resilience and adaptability of both the Tower and the nation it represents, standing as a powerful reminder of the enduring legacy of the past.

Epilogue

Congratulations, young adventurer! You've made it to the end of your journey through the Tower of London. By now, you've uncovered the fascinating stories of kings and queens, knights and ravens, and even a few ghostly tales. You've learned about the great battles, powerful secrets, and strange creatures that once lived inside these ancient stone walls. The Tower of London is a place where every brick seems to have a story, and now, you are part of that story too.

The Tower has stood tall for almost a thousand years, and even today, it continues to amaze everyone who visits. Whether it served as a royal palace, a fortress, a prison, or a place to keep the Crown Jewels safe, the Tower of London is a symbol of England's rich history. Its stories remind us of the bravery, courage, and even the mistakes that shaped the past. And while the times have changed, the Tower still stands, filled with wonders for all who step inside.

As you finish this book, remember that history is all around us. There are still mysteries waiting to be uncovered, treasures to be explored, and legends to be told. The Tower of London is just one of the many incredible stories out there. So, keep exploring, stay curious, and who knows—maybe one day, you'll discover a story of your own to share. Thanks for joining me on this adventure, and may your journey through history never end!

The End.